EXPLORING ENGLISH GRAMMAR IN CONTEXT

| Chunbae Jun |

PUKYONG NATIONAL UNIVERSITY PRESS
부경대학교 출판부

EXPLORING ENGLISH
GRAMMAR IN CONTEXT

2007년 8월 20일 초판1쇄 인쇄
2007년 8월 27일 초판1쇄 발행

저 자 | 전 춘 배
발행인 | 목 연 수
발행처 | 부경대학교 출판부
주 소 | 부산광역시 남구 대연3동 599-1
전 화 | (051) 620-6032
F A X | (051) 626-4554
E-Mail | upress@pknu.ac.kr

값 12,000원

ISBN 978-89-91131-26-2 93740

Preface

Exploring English Grammar in Context is written for intermediate college students of English to expand and solidify their knowledge of English grammar and to use it confidently in speaking, reading, and writing, based on only one fundamental notion that grammatical structures are learned and retained best when they are presented in contexts, that is, on the firm conviction that we learn a great deal about grammar from reading - and not grammar books but newspaper, novels, magazines, even the labels on cereal boxes.

For this purpose and consideration, this text is divided into fourteen parts comprising sixty-eight units. Each part contains grammatically related units with each unit focusing on a specific grammatical form or structure. All units have the same easy-to-follow format, "Grammar Notes" and "Grammatical Exploration in Context":

The Grammar Notes give a brief explanation of the grammar point, focus on the uses, tendencies and meanings of the specific grammatical rules and structures, and are always followed by a variety of examples taken from real language in actual use.

Each Grammatical Exploration in Context with readings that present the unit's grammatical structures is also the part which justifies our title, *Exploring English Grammar in Context,* by exploring grammar in reading contexts. The readings are of a variety of types: newspaper articles extracted chiefly from *The New York Times* and *The USA Today*, sports magazines, stories, autobiographies, and other formats that can be encountered in everyday life.

In addition to reinforcing your understanding of the most important concepts of grammar, usage, and syntax in context, this book will serve to raise student motivation and to provide an opportunity for incidental learning and lively classroom discussions. Topics are varied, ranging from international politics, the weather, employment, the environment, future technology, raising children, sports and traveling, etc.

It is expected that students using this book will be advanced by exploring English grammar through reading contexts in real language in actual use.

Chunbae Jun,
Division of English Language & Literature
Pukyung National University

July 25, 2007

CONTENTS

Adverbs

Moods

Auxiliary verbs

Verbs and passives

Non-finite clauses

Tenses and aspects

The future

Combining clauses

Reporting

Focus and Information processing

EXPLORING ENGLISH GRAMMAR IN CONTEXT

Unit 1 Count and non-count

GRAMMAR NOTES

(1) Classification of nouns

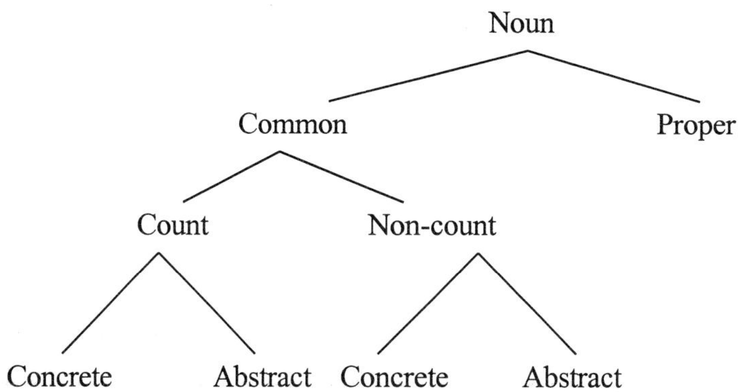

(2) Concrete and abstract nouns

Abstract nouns can be either count or non-count, even though these notions cannot be understood in a physical sense. In general, abstract nouns can more easily be both count and non-count than concrete nouns.

(a) Nouns referring to **events and occasions** (*talk, knock, shot, meeting*, ...) are usually count:

- You've been *a big help*.
- We hope that you will have *a pleasant stay* with us at Imperial Towers.
- I heard a very wise man once say, "Have *a dream* and have *a plan* to make that dream happen."

(b) Other abstract nouns tend to be **non-count only**: *honesty, happiness, information, progress, applause, homework, research*. etc.

- *Freedom* is not free.
- *Wealth* did not bring them *happiness*.

(c) But many such nouns (*experience, difficulty, trouble*, …) can be **either non-count or count** (with some difference of meaning):

- We had considerable *difficulty* finding anywhere to park.
- Tell me about your *experiences* abroad.
- I have some *work* to do this evening.
- They have played two *works* by an unknown French composer.

GRAMMATICAL EXPLORATION IN CONTEXT 

① NOT FOR INDIVIDUAL SALE, Aquafina delivers **a water** so pure, we promise there is nothing but crisp, clean **refreshment** in every bottle. So go ahead and enjoy a great tasting Aquafina.
(**crisp** (adj): pleasantly fresh, cold, and dry)

② The Bush administration hopes the threat of military action will increase the pressure on Iraqi president Saddam Hussein to fully disclose his **efforts** to acquire chemical, biological and nuclear **weapons**.

③ For many travelers, the real **turbulence** begins after **a flight**. Crossing time zones disrupts your body clock and can lead to sleepy days, sleepless nights and malaise. But scientists are learning why **plane travel** throws your body into a tailspin and how to prevent jet lag: Get plenty of **sleep** before your trip and drink water – not alcohol – on the plane.

④ **Snow** might be **a blessing** for skiers and snowboarders, but for Penn State students, it usually means **a** treacherous **walk** to **class**. "I saw a girl take **a** nasty **spill** this morning on Shortlidge," Mike Berda (junior-marketing) said Tuesday. It's pretty icy out."
(**nasty** (adj): unkind or offensive, unpleasant. **spill** (n): a fall from a horse, bicycle, etc.)

⑤ **Sleep** helps keep **memory** and **attention** in top **form**, and it might help regulate **body weight**. **Studies** suggest that **sleep deprivation** is linked to **obesity**, says Meir Kryger, a sleep specialist at the University of Manitoba in Winnipeg, Canada. How much sleep is enough? Most people need seven to nine hours a night, says Kryger, who also is a spokesman for the National Sleep Foundation.
(**in top / rare form**: behaving or performing in a way that is especially clever, skillful, amusing, etc)

Unit 2 Partitives

GRAMMAR NOTES

(1) Partitive constructions:

(det) + (partitive noun) + *of* (non-count / count noun)

- I need *a deck of cards* to show you my new magic trick.
- *A mountain of dirty laundry* was piled up after our vacation.
- There was more than *a grain of truth* in what he'd said.

(2) Partitives by categories

(a) precise **measure** phrases:
a *gallon* of gas, a *yard* of fabric, a *foot* of water, a *yard* of cloth, a *kilo* of flour, an *acre* of land, a *liter* of milk, a *pint* of beer, two *cups* of sugar, two *spoonfuls* of cough syrup, …

(b) **container-based**: a *bottle* of catsup, a *jar* of jam, two *cartons* of books, two *cans* of oil, …

(c) **portion-based**: a *slice* of bread, two *helpings* of potatoes, two *servings* of ice cream, …

(d) **individual members** of a category: *a word of* advice, *an item of* information, *two pieces of* luggage, *two articles of* clothing, …

(e) **parts or fractions**: *a part of* life, *a segment of* society, *two portions of* the budget, *two sections of* the newspaper, …

(f) **shape of**: a *column* of smoke, two *streams* of water, two *sticks* of butter, a *bar* of chocolate, …

(g) **pair of**: *a pair of* trousers / scissors / tongs, …

(h) **quality or subtype**: *a sort of* appliance, *a type of* bird, *new kinds of* media, …

(i) **a majority (minority) of / the whole (rest, remainder) of**

(j) **idiomatic partitives**:

- vegetables: a *stalk* of celery, a *head* of lettuce / cabbage, a *sprig* of parsley, an *ear* of corn, …
- animals: a *herd* of cattle, a *flock* of birds, a *pride* of lions,…
- other food items: a *bunch* of grapes, a *clove* of garlic, a *school* of fish,…
- people: a *gang* of thieves, a *troupe* of actors, a *team* of ball players, a *crew* of helpers, …

GRAMMATICAL EXPLORATION IN CONTEXT

① "We're just **a bunch of** rats. That's how they've been treating us." Earle Young among thousands awaiting rescue outside the Superdome.

② So one day when Nicky was napping I tried on everything in my closet. But **not one single piece of** clothing fit. My butt and boobs were like giant mountains not even the bravest zipper could scale.

(**butt** (n): bottom, **boob** (n): breast, **scale** (v): to climb to or over the top of a high steep object such as a mountain or a wall)

③ **A team of** Japanese scientists reported in Nature magazine in 1967 that it first gave test animals **a dose of** garlic extract and later gave the animals **two shots of** a cancer-causing vaccine. The mice remained free of cancer for nearly four months, they said.

④ A flight from the UK to Portugal over the weekend was forced to make an emergency landing after **a swarm of** bees was sucked into an engine on takeoff. No passengers were injured when the Boeing 737 landed in Bournemoth, although one recounted hearing an "almighty bang" after takeoff. (**recount**: say what happened)

⑤ The family's young children raced on horseback, and their beautiful young mother showed me how to milk a horse. Inside the family's *ger*, every square inch served a purpose. The only sign of modern technology was an old, rusty transistor radio. As is the custom of hospitality in Mongolia, I was offered **a bowl of** fermented mare's milk. (***ger***: kind of tent)

Unit 3 Comparison with nouns

GRAMMAR NOTES

(1) Comparison of gradable countable nouns

The various types of comparison can be applied to gradable countable nouns (like *success, fool, coward*) by the use of *more of a … than, less of a … than, as much of a … as, as little of a … as* etc.:

- How *much of a* fool is he? (= To what extent is he (in your view) a fool?)
- It was *as much / little of a* success *as* I imagined / hoped (it would be).
- He's *too much of a* coward to tell the full story.
- She's *more of a* social animal *than* me.
- I'm *more of a* socialist now *than* before.
- He's *more of a* fool *than* I thought (he was).
- It was *less of a* success *than* I imagined (it would be).
- You're *less of a* fool *than* I thought (you were).
- Getting there is *less of a* problem if you have a car.
- I hope we'll see *more of* you when you've finished your dissertation.
- Please write us and tell us what you'd like to see *more of.* Or let us know what you'd like to see *less of.*
- Parents who readily respond have babies who cry less and who can spend *more of* their energy and time on learning and growing.

(2) Comparison of quantifiers

The quantifiers *much, many, little, few* have special comparative and superlative forms when they function as determiners and pronouns:

- We need *more* money to buy new computers for the students.
- Jack got *more* than he deserved.
- *Most* of our computer equipment is ten years old.
- We also need *more* books in the department.
- I find *most* people working in the library very helpful.
- We now spend *less* money on periodicals than last year.
- I haven't *the least* idea what to do now.

GRAMMATICAL EXPLORATION IN CONTEXT

① Though it seems that many students find text messaging useful, some, like Jason Bender (senior-civil engineering), see it as **more of a** burden.
(**text messaging** = texting: the process of sending and receiving written messages using a cellphone.)

② Isabel raced into Canada on Friday, dumping **less** rain and packing **less of a** punch than expected. By the time it reached the frontier, it had shriveled from a 100 mph hurricane into a 30 mph tropical depression.
(**Isabel**: a name of hurricane. **dump** (v): to drop or let fall in a mass. **pack a punch**: have a strong effect. **shrivel** (v) become weaker or smaller in amount)

③ There's nothing more magical than the expression on your child's face when he's learned something. That's why we've packed our interactive, talking Sort & Soar Rocket with **more** sounds, **more** colors, **more** fun and excitement – all to help develop **more of** your child's abilities.

④ Warnings; keep out of the reach of children under 6 years of age. If **more** than used for brushing is accidentally swallowed, get medical help or contact a Poison Control Center right away.

⑤ Even today in the modern, developed world, surveys show that parents still prefer to have a boy rather than a girl. One long-standing reason why is that boys are expected to become **better** economic providers for their parents' old age. Yet it is time for parents to think again. Girls get **better** grades at school than boys, and in most developed countries **more** women than men go to university. Women will thus be **better** equipped for the new jobs of the 21st century.

Unit 4 Appositives

GRAMMAR NOTES

(1) Restrictive and nonrestrictive appositives: specific identification

- My husband, *a doctor at Queen of Angeles Hospital*, is attending a medical convention in San Francisco.
  (My husband; specifically identified)
- "It is now three months since we gave Saddam what we called a 'final opportunity,'" British Prime Minister *Tony Blair* says.
  (British Prime Minister; not identified specifically)

(2) Types of apposition

(a) Noun + *that*-clause

- *The fact that* they had lied bothered me.
- *The claim* is often made *that* smoking causes heart disease.
- They carried out their *threat* (*that*) they would dismiss workers on strike. (or ···*to dismiss* workers on strike)

(b) Noun + *to*-infinitive

- I accepted Louisa's *invitation to visit* her in New York.
- Provide lots of *opportunities* for your son *to interact* with other kids.

(c) Noun + *of* + *~ing*

- He's got into the habit *of* biting his nails when he's nervous.
- We are exploring the possibility *of* taking legal action against the company.

(d) Noun + *of* + *~ing* / *to*-infinitive

- You have the *option of* bicycling or taking the bus (or ··· the option to bicycle ···)

(e) Noun + *of wh*-clause, *in other words*, etc.

- John raised *the question of when* the money would be collected.
- Our previous meeting looked at *the issue of how to* increase income.
- The mobile library services have been reorganized – *in other words*, they visit fewer places.
- Let your child make some of the small decisions concerning his daily routine. *For instance*, allow him to choose what clothes to wear.

GRAMMATICAL EXPLORATION IN CONTEXT

① In a study released this week, **Marcus Noland, a North Korea expert** at the Institute for International Economics, rated **the chances of the North Korean regime collapsing** at about 3%. North Korea receives about $1 billion a year in foreign aid, Noland says, enough for survival rations for its 22 million people.

② The top American in charge of rebuilding Iraq arrived here today and began **his work of trying to control the violence and breakdown** of civil order that are paralyzing **the American effort to stabilize the country**.

③ **The best way to reduce your child's risk of developing allergies** is to breastfeed her. This is especially true if she's at a higher risk because one of her parents or an older sibling has them.
(if you **develop an illness** or if **it develops**, you become affected by it. **siblings** (n): brothers and sisters.)

④ The White House warned North Korea on Friday that conducting a nuclear test would be "a provocative act," and Japan's foreign minister raised **the possibility of requesting United Nations sanctions against the North**.

⑤ **The renowned Aberdeen ballad-singer, Lizzie Higgins**, died on Saturday in her native city at the age of 63. Lizzie was the daughter of **a very famous mother, the late Jeannie Robertson,** who after her "discovery" in 1953 was acclaimed internationally as the outstanding ballad-singer of modern times. Lizzie's father was **the prize-winning piper Donald Higgins**, whose influence on her musical development complemented that of her mother.

Unit 5 Prepositions after nouns

GRAMMAR NOTES

(1) Nouns + prepositions

(a) nouns + *for*

- Firestone America's *Home for* Car Service.
  (*admiration, check, cure, demand, desire, dislike, lack, need, reason, recipe, respect, responsibility, room, search, sympathy, substitute, taste, thirst, venue,* …)

(b) nouns + *on*

- On Sept. 11, 2001, more than 3,000 people died in terrorist *attacks on* the United States, and by several reckonings, they were all heroes.
  (*agreement, attack, comment, decision, effect, influence, reliance,* …)

(c) nouns + *to*

- Arts and crafts are an ideal *alternative to* television and computer games.
  (*alternative, answer, approach, attitude, contribution, damage, devotion, exception, introduction, invitation, key, marriage, reply, reaction, reference, relevance, resistance, return, solution,* …)

(d) nouns + *with / between*

- Jiang's *meeting with* Bush later this month will probably be his last before stepping down as president.
  (*connection, contact, interview, link, relationship,* …)

(e) nouns + *against*

- He knew it was going to be a hard *fight against* Lewis.
- This is a major victory in the *war against* drugs.

(2) Prepositions + nouns

- Do you want to pay *in cash* or *by credit card*?
- It was simply *by chance* that Nicholson was cast in the movie.
- Our teenagers spend hours *on the phone* every day.
- She's madly *in love* with a guy she met in Spain.
- I can't button my jeans – I'll have to *go on a diet.*
- The whole family *went on a trip to* Hawaii.
- We *went on a 10-day tour of* central Africa.
- Let's *go for a walk* before it gets too hot. (*go on / take* a walk)

GRAMMATICAL EXPLORATION IN CONTEXT 

① And if you have a favorite stamp that you would like to order, especially during the holidays, you can make special **requests for** stamps. We will do everything we can to satisfy your request.

② En route here from Washington, Powell said no **decision on** use of force would be made before President Bush meets British Prime Minister Tony Blair next Friday at Camp David, Md.
(**en route**: on the way: *We happened to be passing through Little Rock en route to Memphis.*)

③ Researchers congratulated the Korean team on improving techniques that might someday be medically useful. Others, including the cloner of Dolly the sheep, renewed their **demand for** a worldwide **ban on** human reproductive cloning.
(**renew** (v): to do something again after a pause, usually with more energy or emphasis than before: *The parties renewed their efforts to sign a peace treaty.*)

④ "There is **discord between** Roh and Bush in that Roh wants to keep providing **aid to** North Korea, while Bush thinks that is not helpful in solving the nuclear issue," said Yu Suk-ryul at the Institute of Foreign Affairs and National Security in Seoul.
(**discord** (n): *formal* disagreement between people)

⑤ While hiring retirees to fill some jobs could be mutually beneficial for the schools and the former educators, it is not the long-term **solution to** staffing problems, Hanna said.
(**staff** (v): to provide an organization with the workers it needs)

Unit 6 Pronouns

GRAMMAR NOTES

(1) The ordering of pronouns

- *You, he and I* will still be at home.
- Why didn't they invite *you and John / you and me / you and her*?
- *He and she* went back to New York.
- *She and another student* came to see me.
- *You and I* should get together sometime and share *our* ideas.
- *You and John* can stop work now. *You* can both eat your lunch in the kitchen.

(2) Anaphoric and cataphoric reference

Cataphoric reference occurs less frequently, and under limited conditions. Where it does occur, anaphoric reference is also possible:

(a) anaphoric reference

- There is *a monster* out there, but is *she* coming to get us here in Central New Jersey? (**monster** = Hurricane Isabel, it **gets me**: to annoy, or attack someone)
- While keeping the left heel grounded during the backswing has several benefits for some golfers, others may not find **this** technique so helpful.

(b) cataphoric reference

- Again, because *they*'re top-heavy, *small children* fall on *their* heads frequently.
- When *they* are behind the wheel, *86% of drivers* say *they* find *themselves* "racing" with other drivers. (**at / behind the wheel**: driving)
- On *his* arrival in the capital, *the Secretary of State* declared support for the government.
- In *his* heyday, *Tom Watson* was probably the best player of the chip shot in the world.

GRAMMATICAL EXPLORATION IN CONTEXT

① **Most** of these expressions are commonly used in conversations among native speakers, and **it** is therefore important for the foreign learner to be familiar with **them** and be able to use **them** quickly, and appropriately, in different situations. Interactive expressions may add little information, but **they** tell **us** something of the speakers' attitude to **their** audience and to what **they** are saying.

② "Has **anybody else** had to watch **their** husband die on television over and over? I know that **it**'s public and I know that **it**'s national, but **it**'s so private for **me**." said the widow of Rick Husband, who died on the space shuttle Columbia.

③ What a horrible thing to see as **my wife, her brother and I** sat in a school parking lot. Child after child of all different sizes struggled to reach the school entrance. **They** were bent over by big backpacks loaded with heavy books. What in heaven do those kids have in these awesome looking bags?

④ Rats carry many potentially life-threatening diseases such as Murine, Typhus, Dysentery, Salmonella, Bubonic Plague and Rabies. A staggering 3.6 million rats are estimated to be born each day. **Each one** is a potential carrier or vector for one or more of the 70 known rat-borne diseases identified so far. **They** jeopardize **our** health and should be considered a serious threat.

⑤ The sooner **you** introduce **your** baby to solid foods, the more likely **she** is to have an allergic reaction. **That**'s why **it**'s best to avoid giving **your** baby solids until **she**'s 6 months old. At that point, **your** pediatrician can guide **you** in gradually introducing solid foods, beginning with **those** that are least likely to cause a reaction, such as rice cereal.

Unit 7 Interrogatives

GRAMMAR NOTES

- *Did Mary leave* town this morning? (Yes-no questions)
- Mom, I'm home. *Where* is everyone? (Wh-questions)
- The boys haven't returned yet, *have they*? (Tag-questions)
- We're going to live in Baguio. *You're going to live where*? (Echo-questions)
- *What* do you think should happen to you?

(1) Choice between interrogative *who* and *whom*

In questions, interrogative *who* is encroaching upon the traditional territory of *whom*. *Who* is much more common than *whom*. This difference is most marked in conversation, where *whom* is virtually non-existent.

(2) After preposition

- To *whom* did you speak? (written)
- "They say that Marlowe was murdered." "By *whom*?"
- For *who*? / From *who*? (conversation)
- "You should give them away." " To *who*?, Spike?"

(3) Stranded prepositions and other positions

When the preposition is stranded at the end of the clause, we find *who* as the regular choice in conversation. In this context, *who* is also normally used in written English. *Who* is also typically used in object position. Less frequently, *whom* is found in these object positions in written English:

- Amanda, *Who* are you going out *with*?
- *Who* did you meet? / Find out *who*?
- "I met a friend of yours on the bus this morning." "Oh, *who*?"
- This is the gentleman *whom* I mentioned a moment ago. (written)

GRAMMATICAL EXPLORATION IN CONTEXT

① **When** you're looking for an apartment, it's a good idea to ask whether it's located in State College Borough, or in Ferguson, Patton, College, Harris or Halfmoon townships. It could affect everything from **what** taxes you can expect to pay to **who** you can go to to report stolen property.

② But, of course, we can never manage to give an adequate written representation of **what** real speech is like. What we can do to get a better idea of real speech – not only of **what** was said, but also **how** it was said – is at least to indicate, as here, the main features of spoken discourse – by far the most widely used form of English.

③ Tell **who** you need to tell, but don't tell everyone. After I had endured a long diagnostic process and calmed myself down, I wondered **whom** to tell and **when** to tell them.

④ You can trust Mr. Handyman for home repairs. There's no shortage of people who want to sell you a new kitchen, new roof or replacement windows. But **who** do you call if you just want to fix The squeaky door? The cracked tile? The broken shelf?

⑤ Respondents to a July Gallup Poll were given the opportunity to name two schools in answer to the question: "All in all, **what** would you say is the best college or university in the United States?" Penn State tied for 11th nationally, with four other schools: the University of Texas, Texas A&M University, Ohio State and the University of North Carolina.

(**all in all**: *mainly spoken* used for showing that you are considering every aspect of something: *All in all, I think it has been a very successful conference.*)

Unit 8 Demonstratives

GRAMMAR NOTES

(1) Demonstratives *this* / *these* have a sense of "nearness" and *that* / *those* a sense of "distance". The nearness or distance could be spatial, temporal, psychological, or simply sequential (*this* = first mention vs. *that* = second mention):

- *This* is my towel and *that*'s yours. (spatial)
- I like *this* movie better than *that* concert last night. (temporal)
- I like *this* candidate, which is why I didn't vote for *that* one. (psychological)
- *This* dress is less attractive than *that* one. (sequential)

(2) Demonstratives can have **three different uses**; *exophoric*, *anaphoric* and *cataphoric*.

(a) exophoric (reference to people and things outside the text)

- Is *this* your first visit to Wyoming?
- Would you like to sit in *this* chair or in *that* one?

(b) anaphoric (backward pointing)

- I then tried to force the door open, but *this* / *that* was a mistake.
- It was a secret – *that*'s why they never talked about it.
- Sometimes there's flooding, and *this* is why no one wants to live here.

(c) cataphoric (forward pointing)

- Now, *this* is what I want you to do, so listen carefully.
- *This* is how you start a car: you make sure the gears are in neutral and that the hand brake is on, then turn the ignition key.

(3) cataphoric *it* as a clause substitution

We can use a pattern with *it* ··· as the object of a verb where *it* refers forward to a *that-*, *if-*, or *when-clause* after *can't bear, hate, like, love, resent* and *can't stand*, and to an *if-* or *when-clause* after *dislike, enjoy, prefer* and *understand*:

- We always *enjoy it when* they stay with us.
- I *hate it that* you can swim so well and I can't.
- We always *like it when* you stay with us.
- I *love it* when she dances. She moves to gracefully.
- I would *appreciate it* if you would just let me deal with this.

GRAMMATICAL EXPLORATION IN CONTEXT 

① At mealtime, I often tell my son that if he eats all of his vegetables, he'll grow up to be healthy and strong. Then I smile, because **that**'s exactly what my mom used to say to me.

② With the acceptance of six refugees, the United States has opened a new era for North Korean asylum-seekers. **This** is the first time North Koreans have been granted refugee status by the United States.

③ The surgery was first reported by the *San Francisco Chronicle.* The newspaper reported Bonds would take antibiotics for at least two weeks and could not resume his rehab until doctors are assured the infection is gone. "It's the third time that he's going to be out longer, so we are accustomed to **that** now," Giants manager Felipe Alou said after a 6-2 loss at Arizona on Wednesday.
(**Barry Bonds**: a baseball super star at American Giants Team)

④ Golfers tend to build up the importance of certain shots, most commonly the first tee shot or the last few shots in a good round. **This** is why you generally feel more nervous on the first tee than at any other time during a round: you have put yourself under unnecessary pressure. **This** is the main reason why some golfers hit poor opening drives.

⑤ Prevention is also needed in skin whitening. Sekkisei Recovery Essence Excellent is a whitening essence that helps the skin recover from accumulated sun damage while preventing the dark spots and wrinkles associated with aging. I **love that** the pink essence not only smelled good but it also replenished the essential moisture that my skin needed to stay nourished and hydrated.

Unit 9 Reflexives

GRAMMAR NOTES

(1) Coreference

The reflexive pronouns are always coreferential with a noun or another pronoun, agreeing with it in gender, number, and person:

- I'll do it *myself.*
- The dog was scratching *itself.*
- He and his wife poured *themselves* a drink.
  cf. He and his wife poured *them* a drink.
- I hope the children behave *themselves.*

(2) The coreference must be within the same clause.

- Penelope begged Jane to look after *her.* (= Penelope)
- Penelope begged Jane to look after *herself.* (= Jane)

(3) Reflexive verbs

A few transitive verbs require subject and object are coreferential:

- They *availed themselves of* the opportunity to hear a free concert.
- They *pride themselves on* their well-kept garden. (*absent ⋯ from, avail ⋯ of, busy ⋯ with, concern ⋯ with, help ⋯ to, occupy ⋯ with, pride ⋯ on, ⋯*)

(4) Preposition + reflexive pronoun

- He was *pleased with himself.* (*be ashamed of, feel sorry for, be proud of, be pleased with, ⋯*)
- The old lady sat in a corner *talking to herself.*
- As your loved ones get older, they may become weak, sick or otherwise unable to *care for themselves.* (*believe in, care about, do with, hear about, look after, look at, take care of, talk to, ⋯*)
- I remember closing the door *behind me.*
- Take some money *with you* in case you need it.

GRAMMATICAL EXPLORATION IN CONTEXT

① If he wants to feed **himself** but you don't have all day to wait for him to get an ounce of food in, give him one spoon to feed **himself** while you use another to get most of the meal into his mouth.

② First of all, even in the U.S., cigarettes have been branded as a harmful commodity on the level of narcotics, and smoking **itself** has been gradually banned from most public places.

(**narcotics** (n): (often plural) any illegal drug)

③ So a lot of the time, we just didn't talk at all. We **threw ourselves into** our jobs and **devoted ourselves to** our daughter, and when we didn't have either of those distractions, we went to sleep.

(**distraction** (c): an activity that you can do for fun or entertainment)

④ The Vivaldi Italian Restaurant serves some of the finest Italian cuisine in town. **Treat yourself to** a great selection of seafood, pastas and pizzas for lunch and dinner, with a unique Italian flair.

⑤ Until last week, North Korea had never boasted about its nuclear weapons capability, insisting it was only interested in producing electric power from nuclear reactors. The change in tactics, the administration's Korea experts believe, may be an effort to raise the price of dismantling its program, if President Bush **reversed himself** and was willing to strike a deal to disarm the country.

(**reverse *oneself***: to change a decision you have made. **strike (make) a deal / bargain**: to make something such as a deal or an agreement)

Unit 10 *One* and *ones*

GRAMMAR NOTES

(1) the use of *one* and *ones*

- This knife is too blunt. I must buy a sharper *one.*
- The clean towels are in the drawer – if you need *one.* (= a clean towel)
- I'd never seen a game like *that one.*
- If you need any more paper, I'll bring you *some.* (* ··· some one / ones)
- Have you got any lemons? I need *one / some* for a meal I'm cooking.
- They were all dealing drugs, but Bob was *the one* who got caught.
- I think his best poems are his early *ones.*
- Mr. Linden's experiences with his son are *ones* that are shared by countless other parents.
- We need new curtains. Okay, let's buy green *ones* this time.
- We need new curtains. Okay, let's buy *some.* (* ··· let's buy *ones*)
- The clothes shop on the corner has re-opened as a *shoe shop.* (* ··· a shoe one ···)
- The shoe is crafted to feel more like *an athletic shoe* than *a dress shoe.*

(2) the possibility of ellipsis of *one* and *ones*

We can leave out *one / ones* after *which, superlatives, this, that, these, those, either, neither, another, each, the first / second / last* etc. but not after *the, the only, the main, every,* and adjectives. However, after *color* adjectives we can often leave out *one / ones* in answers:

- Timson has made 13 films and I think *her latest* is *the best.*
- Look at that pumpkin! It's *the biggest* (*one*) I've seen this year.
- There are two small ponds just in front of the tees and *another* to the right that can capture a sliced drive.
- When you cook clams you shouldn't eat *the ones* that don't open.
- My shoes were so uncomfortable that I had to go out today and buy some *new ones.*
- "Have you decided which jumper to buy?" "Yes, I think I'll take the *blue* (*one*)."

GRAMMATICAL EXPLORATION IN CONTEXT

① The development of modern drugs is hard, costly and fraught with risk. It is said to take at least a decade and hundreds of millions of dollars to create **a new one**, and many such attempts fail between the test tube and the clinic. (**fraught with sth**: full of problems, difficulties, or things that are confusing.

② My thanks to Michael Swan for a number of good ideas; also to many colleagues, students and friends, who have both suggested new activities and provided practical, constructive criticisms of **old ones.**

③ I was reading that book, "The Great Fire," at a downtown coffee joint when a friend happened in and looked over my shoulder. " Is it fiction?" he asked. "Or is it dry fact after dry fact?" "It's **neither one**." I said, incensed. "It's an exciting true story that is well-told."
(**joint** (n): *informal* a restaurant, bar, or club, especially one that is inexpensive and not very nice.
incensed (adj): extremely angry)

④ Soon you'll begin seeing the newly designed U.S. currency, with subtle background colors and enhanced security features. But one thing will never change: The old bills will always be worth just as much as **the new**. All bills are good.

⑤ You can find drug stores on any street corner. But **the ones** listed below are **the best** in town and will find time to be friendly and helpful. If you're from abroad, they will also be able to 'translate' your non-American drug into its local equivalent.

Unit 11 Determiners

GRAMMAR NOTES

(1) Classes of determiners

(a) central determiners

articles (*a, the, zero*), demonstratives (*this, that, these, those*) possessives (*my, our, your, his, her, its, their*), *wh*-determiners (*which, whose, whichever, whatever, whosever*), quantifiers (*no, every, each, either, neither, some, any, enough, much*)

(b) predeterminers

all, both, half, what, such, multipliers (*twice, double, three times,* ···), fractions,

(c) postdeterminers

a. numerals (*one, two, three,* ··· *first, second, third,* ··· *next, last, other, further,* ···)

b. quantifiers (*three, sixty, many, few, a lot of, plenty of,* ···)

- *The* area is approximately *three times the* size of the old location.
- He said goodbye to *his many* friends.
- At first glance *the* idea looked *such a* good one.

(2) Specific vs. non-specific

Indefinite determiners can be divided into *specific* indefinites and *non-specific* indefinites. In the case of a specific indefinite, the speaker has a specific instance in mind; in the case of non-specific indefinites, an arbitrary instance is 'conjured up' for the immediate purpose at hand. The indefinite determiner *a* and unstressed *some* and *any* can be used in either specific or non-specific reference.

- There was *a child* playing in the park. (specific)
- You need *an egg* for this recipe. (non-specific)
- There were *some children* playing in the park. (specific)
- You need *some milk* for this recipe. (non-specific)
- John wanted to marry *a rich woman* though he didn't know *her* well.
- John wanted to marry *a rich woman* though he didn't know *any* (well)
- John wanted to marry *the rich woman* he met on a cruise, though he didn't love *her* / **any.*

GRAMMATICAL EXPLORATION IN CONTEXT 

① During **the** past 60 years, nearly **every** family in America has sent one or more of **their** sons and daughters to fight somewhere in defense of freedom. Don't you think that **the** very least we owe them is adequate medical care provided in **a** timely manner? (**owe someone something**: to think you should treat someone in a particular way)

② **The** no's came mostly from people who supported **the** idea of breast-feeding but felt that it should be done privately because it could be embarrassing to **both the** mother and **an** onlooker, says Sarah Smith, **a** senior associate editor who oversees **the** monthly surveys.

③ ***All My*** *Children* was created by Agnes Nixon. Although Nixon had previously created *One Life to Live* for ABC following her success as head writer for *Another World*, ***All My*** *Children* was **her first** love and first major creation. She set the show in Pine Valley, Pennsylvania, a small suburb of Philadelphia.

④ Clinton is scheduled to make **his first** public appearance as a U.N. envoy Wednesday. He is to meet with Secretary General Kofi Annan for **the first** time since his appointment was announced on Feb. 1, and they will hold a news conference, U.N. spokesman Stephane Dujarric announced Friday.

⑤ Even after four decades, I can vividly recall the emotions felt by everyone in that crowd of a quarter-million people filling the Mall and stretching back toward the Capitol, as King stood at the feet of Abraham Lincoln at the memorial to the Great Emancipator and filled the air with his vision of a nation where "**my four little** children will one day live in a nation where they will not be judged by the color of their skin but by the content of their character." (**the Great Emancipator** = Abraham Lincoln)

Unit 12 *Some* and *any*

GRAMMAR NOTES

The primary difference between *some* and *any* (and between the *some-* and *any-*compounds) is that *some* is **specific**, though unspecified, while *any* is **nonspecific**. That is, *some* implies an amount or number that is known to the speaker. This difference tends to correlate with the difference between positive and negative contexts.

(1) *Some*

- Are there *some* letters for me?
- She married *some* guy she met on the boat.
- What's wrong? Have you got *something* in your eye?
- A: What would you like to drink?
  B: Well, if I could have *something* I like, I think I'd choose *some* really cold milk.
- *Some* people like pigeons and *some* don't.
- *Some* people never send *any* Christmas cards.
- You can't learn English *unless* you make *some* mistakes.
  cf. You can't learn English *if* you do*n't* make *any* mistakes.

(2) *Any*

- There aren't *any* classes today.
- Do you have *any* money?
- If *anyone* has *any* questions, I'll be pleased to answer them.
- Without *any* hesitation at all, Jane came forward to volunteer.
- If *any* member of the team was sick, Gary would take his place.
- It's a very simple test – *any* idiot could pass it.
- *Any* person allergic to fish products should consult with a physician before taking this product.
- We can't go ahead with the meeting, because very few people have shown *any* interest.

(3) *Some* and *any* in the scope of negation

- I didn't attend *some* of the lectures. (= I attended *some* of the lectures.)
- I didn't attend *any* of the lectures. (= I attended *none* of the lectures.)

GRAMMATICAL EXPLORATION IN CONTEXT

① **Anyone** who's driven through the American countryside knows how limited radio options are in much of the country.

② Welcome to New Brunswick's Guide to Dining, Entertainment and Select Shops. Whether you are a long-time resident or a first time visitor, there is always **something** new and exciting to discover in New Brunswick.

③ Drop 10 balls around a green. Make a point of varying the quality of the lie. Place **some** on the closely mown apron of the green and others in the first cut of rough (with a few sitting up and **some** nestling down).
(**make a point of ~ing** = make it a point to …= be sure to, mow - mowed - mowed / **mown**. **rough** (n): the part of a golf course where the grass is tall and not cut.)

④ After a wide-ranging interview with The Times in which he sharply denied that he had done **anything** in his career that could be counted as a crime against humanity, Gen. Zuhayr Naqib, the director of military intelligence under Hussein, surrendered to U.S. forces here.

⑤ Finding a place to live is no small project. After you decide whether it's more reasonable to rent or own, you have to pore over the classifieds and do **some** serious legwork until you finally come across **something** that fits.
(**pore over sth**: to examine or read something very carefully and in a lot of detail. **legwork** (n): *informal* tiring or boring work that you have to do as a part of a job, for example collecting information from different places.)

Unit 13 *Much* and *many*

GRAMMAR NOTES

(1) Nonassertive *much* and *many*

Much and, to a lesser extent, *many* have acquired some nonassertive force, with the result that they are rarely used, at least in informal English, without some negative or interrogative implication.

- We have endured *?much* / We have endured *a great deal.*
- She has *many* good ideas.
- She has *plenty of / a lot of* good ideas.

(2) *Much* and *many* in affirmative sentences

In affirmative sentences we generally use *a lot of* and *lots (of)* rather than *much (of)* and *many (of)*, particularly in informal context. However, there are a number of exceptions;

(a) In formal contexts, such as academic writing, *much (of)* and *many (of)* are often preferred:
- There could be *many* explanations for this.
- *Much* debate has been heard about Thornton's new book.

(b) We usually use *many* rather than *a lot of* or *lots of* with time expressions (*minutes, days. weeks, months, years*) and number + *of* (e.g. *thousands of* voters, *millions of* pounds):
- We used to spend *many* hours driving to New Brunswick and back.
- He was the founder of a company now worth *many* millions of pounds.

(c) In both formal and informal contexts we can use *much* and *many* in affirmative sentences after *as, so,* and *too*:
- I'd say there were twice *as many* women at the meeting *as* men.
- It didn't hurt *as much as* last time.
- Thanks *so much* for including "Getting a Grip" in your November issue.
- I was excited to see *so many* pretty pieces of lingerie until I glanced at the prices.
- *Too many* people still smoke.
- He drinks *too much.*

GRAMMATICAL EXPLORATION IN CONTEXT

① In a home-fall emergency, **many** seniors can**not** reach the telephone. They remain on the floor for hours or even days without any help.

② Snacking isn't a dirty word, especially for toddlers. They have tiny stomachs, so they ca**n't** eat **much** at each meal and need two to three snacks a day.

③ Health care costs didn't hurt employers as much as had been forecast this year, mainly because **so many** shifted costs to their employees, according to a survey out Monday.
(**so many**: so many (employers), **shift** (v): to move slightly)

④ At least five deaths had been blamed on the weather since snow burst across the Plains on Friday and Saturday. "This is looking like the largest storm this year, and it may be one of the top five in our recorded history," said Lora Rakowski of Maryland's Highway Administration. "You name a place, they've got snow - and **a lot of** it."
(**blame A on B** : B is responsible for A (an accident, problem, or bad situation)

⑤ "I use text messages when I have something quick to say that doesn't really require **a lot of** explanation or a whole phone call," Krupski said. "I also use text messages if I want to give a quick hello to someone and don't have **a lot of** time to talk."
(**text message**: a written message that you send or receive using a cellphone.)

Unit 14 Genitives

GRAMMAR NOTES

(1) Choice between *of*-construction and *'s* genitive

- What's *the ship's name*? / What's *the name of the ship*?
- *The child's bicycle* was smashed to bits. (← The child had a bicycle.)
- The police didn't believe *Mary's story*. (← Mary told a story.)
- She was upset by *that neighbor's murder*. (← Somebody murdered that neighbor.)
- *The roof of the house* blew off during the big storm.
- She is *the sister of someone* I used to go to school with.
- Moms share their secrets for making every day seem like *Valentine's Day* .
- The army defeated the rebels.
  → the army's defeat of the rebels / the defeat of the rebels by the army
- The rebels were defeated by the army.
  → the rebels' defeat by the army

(2) 'double' genitive

- He's *a brother of Leda's* (Leda has more than one brother)
  cf. He's *Leda's brother*. (Leda has one, or more than one, brother)
- *An idea of yours* has been adopted by the boss.
- *An admirer of my mother's* sent her a dozen roses.
- I can't stand *those cats of Susan's*. / cf. I can't stand *Susan's cats*.
- *That music of Stan's* is simply awful.
- *The friend of mine* who gave me this dress wants it back.

(3) Genitive without a head noun

The noun modified by the *'s* genitive may be omitted, if the context makes its identity clear. When the *of*-construction is used instead, a pronoun (*that* or *those*) is usually required.

- My car is faster than *John's*. (than *John's* car)
- We met at *Johnson's*. (house / store, etc.)
- I must go to *the butcher's* (*chemist's*) / *butcher* (*chemist*) this morning.
- *A blind person's sense of touch* is more sensitive to shape and size than *that of a person with normal vision*.
- The new CD players are much better than *those of the first generation*.

GRAMMATICAL EXPLORATION IN CONTEXT

① J.K. Rowling, who became **the world's** first billion dollar author on the back of **Harry Potter's** success, has given the go-ahead for **the creation of a Florida theme park** dedicated to the schoolboy wizard. "This plans I have seen look incredibly exciting and I don't think **fans of the books and films** will be disappointed," Rowling said of the Orlando park that is scheduled to open in 2009. (**on the back of sth**: because of something, or helped by something. **give / get the go-ahead**: to give / get the permission to do something.)

② **The British government's introduction of a new and advanced biometric system** for visa applicants in the Philippines is not aimed at Filipinos illegally staying in the United Kingdom.

③ Without a doubt, most vacationers should seriously consider travel insurance. A variety of options are available to satisfy **the needs of many different travelers**. If you don't know where to begin, here are some answers to commonly asked questions.

④ And that includes not only **the evacuation of the Japanese nationals** or **the protection of Japanese oil tankers**, but probably **the post-war rehabilitation of Iraq** as well as **the support and rescue of the refugees**.

⑤ If you're like most of us, falling in love with a pet is easy. And no wonder! Sharing your home with a four-legged friend can be one of **life's greatest joys.** Dogs, cats, and other pets give us unconditional loyalty and acceptance, provide constant companionship, and even help relieve stress after **a hard day's work**.

Unit 15 Adjectives

GRAMMAR NOTES

(1) Attributive — predicative

- The *full* moon shone brightly. (attributive)
- The moon is *full* tonight. (predicative)
- She's our *chief* economic advisor. (attributive only)
- She was the *former* prime minister.
- I'm *afraid* I don't really agree with that, Bill. (predicative only)
- I'm very *fond* of Hemingway.

(2) Stative — dynamic

- He's being *careful.* Be *careful.* / Please be *considerate* of others.
  cf. *He's being *tall.* *Be *tall.*
- I didn't realize he was being *funny.* Her story was very *funny.*
  (dynamic adjectives; *brave, calm, cheerful, conceited, cruel, foolish, friendly, funny, good, greedy, helpful, jealous, naughty, noisy, tidy,* etc.)

(3) Adjunct adjectives: adjectives that function as adjuncts

Sometimes intransitive verbs are followed by adjectives that modify the subject (a) by indicating what state it is in (b) by specifying a resultant state.

- Charley sleeps *nude.* / They emerged from the building *alive.*
- Mary arrived *drunk.* / Cassie walked into the room *mad.*
  cf. Mary arrived *while she was drunk.*
- The river froze *solid* / The box broke *open* / A door slammed *shut.*

(4) The intensifiers *good and* and *nice and*

Good and or *nice and* often serve to intensify the degree of the second adjective. In both AmE and BrE conversation, *nice and* is far more frequent than *good and.*

- "Shall we get some strawberries?" "Yes, they look *nice and* fresh." (*nice and* warm / bright / clean / cold / comfortable / early / fresh / quiet / simple, …)
- Good for your teeth. Makes your teeth *nice and* strong!
- If you're all feeling *good and* relaxed after the break, let's get on with the meeting. (*good and* ready / proper / relaxed / strong / warm, etc.; *informal.* completely ready, …)

GRAMMATICAL EXPLORATION IN CONTEXT

① There are numerous drills for a variety of pre-swing and in-swing corrections, but I will focus on a **select** few that will fortify your pre-swing and in-swing foundations, but most importantly – these can be done at home! (**select**(adj): carefully chosen om a larger group, **a select few**, cf. **the chosen few**: elite)

② Children want to work with us. They love to clean, cook and garden with us. Children are **happiest** when they are doing important things with the people who are **most important** to them.

③ American soldiers gathered **the dead**, placing the bodies in black bags and leaving them beside the road before moving on. They also collected the dead soldiers' belongings, one officer said, so that word could be passed to their families.
(**belongings** (n): possessions. **word** (n): (non-count) If there is **word** of something, people receive news or information about it. *No Word has come from home.*)

④ Breastfeeding is **best** but if you are unable or choose not to, then the formula you select should be as close as possible to breast milk. Talk to your doctor about which formula is **best** for your baby.
(**choose** (v): to want, like, or decide. **formula** (n): baby milk. **close to**: similar to)

⑤ Basic photo albums can be purchased cheaply at many stores. Get **the plainest, most basic** album you can find. Once you find the one you want, it is time to personalize it. (**personalize** (v): to make or change something so that it is especially appropriate for a particular person)

Unit 16 Adjective order

GRAMMAR NOTES

(1) When two or more adjectives co-occur in attributive position, the order of the adjectives is to a large extent determined by their **semantic properties**;

Determiners + general + specific +
opinion adjective
size + shape + condition + age + color + origin + Noun
descriptive adjective

- a *tall young* woman
- a *plump dark-haired* child
- *fresh green* onions
- an *old, brown, leather* briefcase
- The *poor little pink plastic* doll
- two *beautiful brown Greek* ceramic water pitchers
- a *funny old red Spanish* leather riding boots
- An *ugly big round chipped old blue French* vase

(2) Attributive adjectives are sometimes conjoined with *and* when there are **two adjectives from the same category** that both partially modify the same noun.

- an *orange and white* marble / a *wooden and metal* implement
- So here are four key products from the Sekkisei Excellent series for snowy *white and bright* skin.

(3) Certain adjectives have a **variable order**: proper adjectives and adjectives of material (*wooden, brick, glassy*), proper adjectives and adjectives of color, and adjectives denoting shape (*round, oblong, wide, flat*) in combination with other adjectives, may be rearranged according to the demands of the context:

- These *Japanese wooden /wooden Japanese* chests
- A large *Chinese porcelain / porcelain Chinese* vase
- a *small / blue round* table
- a *round blue / small* table

GRAMMATICAL EXPLORATION IN CONTEXT

① Now we felt the emotional resonance of **the beautiful traditional Gaelic** greeting: *Cead mile failte* – "One hundred thousand welcomes."

② While Mr. Ahmadinejad was enjoying **a warm public** welcome in Shanghai, U. S. and European diplomats at **the International Atomic** Energy in Vienna tried to press Iran to halt **sensitive nuclear** activities that could produce material for atomic bombs.

③ By the time I crossed the threshold of the White House, I had been shaped by my family upbringing, education, religious faith and all that I had learned before – as the daughter of **a staunch conservative** father and a more liberal mother, a student activist, an advocate for children, a lawyer, Bill's wife and Chelsea's mom.

④ The islands include almost 70% of **the nation's tropical, shallow-water** coral reefs, a rookery for 14 million seabirds and the last refuge for **the endangered Hawaiian** monk seal and **the threatened green** sea turtle. The area also has an abundance of **large predatory** fish at a time when 90% of such species have disappeared from the world's oceans.

⑤ One year it was a pocket-size transistor radio I craved. They were the newest thing, and I started by opening the smallest packages. No radio. Then the medium-sized ones. I began to fear Santa hadn't got my letter. Finally, in **a** package **large and rectangular** enough to be clothes, was my prize. A blue radio with an ear plug. Santa is **a clever old** guy!
(**crave (for)**: (= long for) to want something very much and in a way that is very hard to control)

Unit 17 Participle adjectives

GRAMMAR NOTES

(1) **Participle adjectives**: some ~*ing* forms (present participles) and ~*ed* forms (past participle) of verbs can be used as adjectives:
- The *proposed* new regulation is not compatible with our *existing* policy.
- My mother seemed *delighted* with the present.

(2) Often **the difference between the adjective and the participle** is not clear cut. The verbal force of the participle is explicit for the ~*ing* form when a direct object is present, and for the ~*ed* form when a *by*-agent with a personal agent is present:
- You are *frightening* the children.
- Her views were *alarming* her audience.
- The man was *offended* by the policeman.
- She was *misunderstood* by her parents.

(3) For both participle forms, **premodification by the intensifier *very*** is an explicit indication that the forms have achieved adjective status:
- Her views were very *alarming*.
- You are very *frightening*.
- The man was very *offended*.

(4) Generally, ~*ed* participle forms accepting *very* can retain *very* when they cooccur with a ***by*-phrase containing a nonpersonal noun phrase** that expresses the notion of *cause* or *reason*:
- I'm *very* disturbed by your attitude.
- We were *very* pleased by his behavior.

(5) Some verbs have **different past participle forms** for verbal and adjectival use:
- You have *drunk* too much. ~ *drunk*(*en*) driving / driver
- Have you *shaved*? ~ a clean-*shaven* young man
- The shirt has *shrunk*. ~ a *shrunken* shirt

GRAMMATICAL EXPLORATION IN CONTEXT 

① "We're **very encouraged** by indications that North Korea is accepting our proposals for multilateral talks," State Department spokesman Richard Boucher said.

② European Union governments may soon issue passports **containing** computer chips **embedded** with digital fingerprints or eye scans, according to a plan **approved** by European leaders today.

③ A top bird flu expert on Tuesday predicted that the H5N1 virus would not reach the United States this year via migratory birds, but he warned it would eventually arrive, possibly through **infected** birds **smuggled** into the country.

④ Establishing the Northwestern Hawaiian Islands as a strictly **protected** marine reserve, could prove to be the Bush administration's most **enduring** environmental legacy

⑤ Philadelphia schools, with about 12,000 teachers, generally carry about 100 vacancies; additionally, the system hires hundreds of people each year who lack full credentials for classroom spots. This year, 60 percent of the 600 new teachers **hired** had emergency credentials, meaning they had not passed state certification tests or had not taken all the **required** education courses.

Unit 18 Compound adjectives

GRAMMAR NOTES

(1) A compound adjective consists of two or more words together used as an adjective. Many compound adjectives include a **participle adjective**. Common patterns are:

noun / adjective / adverb + ~*ed* / ~*ing* participle.

- I hope it will be a *money-making* enterprise.
- An *energy-saving* bulb consumes 80% less energy and lasts up to 10 times longer than a standard bulb.
- The public square was *tree-lined.*
- She seems to live on *ready-made* frozen meals.
- He is the *longest-serving* employee in the company.
- An *important-looking* letter arrived for Dave.
- They are *well-behaved* (children).
- He wants *home-cooked* meals.
- These are all *hard-working* students.
- China's economic boom is generating a *fast-growing* market at home.

(2) We can use **some participle adjectives *only* in adjective compounds**. For example, we can't say '… *behaved* children' or '… a *making* enterprise' as the sense is incomplete without the adverb or noun. Other compounds like this include *London-based, Paris-born, heart-breaking, brick-built, easy-going, peace-keeping, long-lasting, good-looking, home-made, hair-raising, far-reaching, well-dressed, sweet-smelling, strange-sounding, soft-spoken, sour-tasting, nerve-wracking.*

(3) Many other compound adjectives do not include participle adjectives:
- We've just bought a *brand-new* car.
- I'm sure we could offer you some *short-term* employment.
- It was just a *small-scale* project.
- Is that a *new-style* cardigan?
- Emma has some pretty *old-fashioned* notions.

GRAMMATICAL EXPLORATION IN CONTEXT

① Nestled on the side of Mt. Nittany, in the heart of central Pennsylvania, is a small, **family-owned** winery producing **award-winning** wines sold throughout the state.

② On the White House lawn, President Bush bowed his head in silence at 8:46 a.m., the moment that the first **terrorist-hijacked** plane struck the World Trade Center.

③ Washington believes North Korea has one or two atomic bombs and may be trying to make more. The North has disputed that claim, saying its nuclear program is meant to generate **much-needed** electricity.

④ "I want to emphasize to the people that there is no military threat in Iraq that can drive us out," Abizaid said. "We have the **best-equipped, best-trained** army in the world positioned in the most difficult areas we have to deal with ... They are confident, they are capable, they know what they are doing."
(**drive out**: force someone or something to leave a place. **deal with sth**: to take action to do something, especially to solve a problem)

⑤ "We are the best value in Asia and the best place to invest in Asia," President Arroyo said. "We offer a strategic location in **a fast growing** region. Our workforce is **well educated**, productive and **English speaking**. We are cutting red tape to simplify the requirements for investing in the Philippines."

Unit 19 Prepositions after adjectives

GRAMMAR NOTES

(1) adjectives + *of*

- President Bush said he's *'sick and tired' OF* Saddam Hussein's deception. (*aware, capable, certain, conscious, critical, full, incapable, short, sure, suspicious, tired, tolerant, typical,* ⋯)
- Other girls were *jealous OF* her good looks. (*afraid, frightened, terrified / ashamed, envious, fond, jealous, proud,* ⋯)

(2) adjectives + *to*

- All these factors are *extraneous TO* our objectives. (*accustomed, adjacent, allergic, available, close, due, engaged, grateful, identical, married, opposed, preferable, related, resistant, similar, subject, susceptible, vital,* ⋯)

(3) adjectives + *with*

- The president declared himself *satisfied WITH* the progress of the talks. (*acquainted, bored, compatible, crowded, delighted, disappointed, familiar, filled, friendly, happy, pleased, satisfied,* ⋯)

(4) adjectives + *for*

- You could be *eligible FOR* a university scholarship. (*answerable, eligible, famous, grateful, necessary, responsible, sorry, suitable, thankful,* ⋯)

(5) adjectives + *from*

- It's not much *different FROM* cracking an egg. Once the shell is broken, you can't put it back together. (*different, distant, distinct, free,*) (*different than* (AmE) / *to* (BrE))

(6) adjectives + *on / upon*

- They hate being dependent *ON / UPON* their parents. (*based, dependent, keen, set,* ⋯)

(7) adjectives + *at*

- I am hopeless *AT* paying my bills on time. (*alarmed, amazed, astonished, bad, brilliant, clever, excellent, good, hopeless, surprised,* ⋯)

(8) adjectives + *about*

- We are very worried *ABOUT* our future. (*angry, anxious, annoyed, excited, furious, reasonable, upset, worried,* ⋯)

GRAMMATICAL EXPLORATION IN CONTEXT

① It needn't come to that. Iran's leaders may see that a growing economy and supportive populace is more **vital to** maintaining their regime than Iran becoming a nuclear-capable military power.

② Q: How can I prevent my newborn from developing food allergies?

A: You're smart to start planning now. Some babies are very **susceptible to** food allergies, and there are experts who feel that what you feed your infant can also affect his chances of developing them later in life.

(**susceptible to**: easily influenced or affected by something: Police officers here are very susceptible to corruption.)

③ A recent large-scale study, called the Diabetes Prevention Program, found that losing weight and increasing physical activity can help those **prone to** diabetes reduce the risk of developing the disease by 58 percent. (**prone to**: likely to do something or be affected by something, especially something bad)

④ Consumer spending soared, foreigners bought American-made goods at a surprising clip and companies increased their investments in equipment and technology at a pace **reminiscent of** the 1990's boom.

(**at a fast / good / surprising clip**: *informal* quickly. **reminiscent of**: reminding you of people and experiences in your past)

⑤ "I think we made some very, very good progress on the very important issues of Iraq debt," Mr. Baker told reporters after his meeting with Mr. Koizumi. "Prime Minister Koizumi and Japan have taken a leadership role in the reconstruction of Iraq, something that is extraordinarily important and **for** which the United States is very **grateful**." (**grateful for** = thankful for. *I'm very grateful for all your help with the party.*)

Unit 20 Adverbs

GRAMMAR NOTES

(1) Types of adverbs

- We have to preserve these buildings *before it's too late.*
- We meet for lunch *once a week.* (temporal adverb)
- It *hardly ever* rains here in the summer.
- The baby's *almost* walking now. (adverb of frequency)
- If you look *in the top drawer*, you'll probably find it *there.*
- I was sick on the plane *home.* (adverb of place)
- The baby crawled *up the stairs.*
- They waded *into the water.* (adverb of direction)
- She spoke *confidently / in a confident manner / with confidence.*
- He skis *like a professional.* (adverb of manner)
- I always commute *by subway.*
- This garment was made *by hand.* (adverb of means)
- The program failed *because of a software error.*
- We ran *for cover.* (adverb of reason / purpose)
- They responded *very* enthusiastically.
- The dog ate *quite* greedily. (degree adverb)
- You can come, *only* make sure you're on time.
- It will rain today, *particularly* in the north. (focus adverb)
- *Consequently,* Mary had to find another babysitter.
- *Fortunately*, it didn't rain the day of our picnic. (sentence adverb)

(2) Forms of adverbs

- A friend of mine has *very kindly* offered to baby-sit. (adverb phrase)
- What are you doing *this afternoon*? (NP)
- I found several people waiting *outside the doctor's door.* (PP)
- We have to preserve these buildings *before it's too late.* (finite clause)
- As usual, Peter was playing *to win.* (infinitive clause)
- I used to lie awake at night, *worrying about the next exam.*
- Two people were found dead, *presumably killed by cars.*
- The actor admitted to driving *while under the influence of drink.*

GRAMMATICAL EXPLORATION IN CONTEXT

① To teach your child, hold up the card, say the word out **loud** then, ask your child to repeat it. Big, bold letters and delightful illustrations make learning fun!

② Canada's Senate late Tuesday voted to adopt landmark legislation to legalize gay marriage **nationwide** despite fierce opposition from Conservatives and religious leaders. The bill could be signed into law as **early** as Wednesday. (**landmark** (adj) (only before noun): important and likely to influence future actions. **gay** (adj): homosexual, mainly used about men. cf. lesbian)

③ In a Harris Interactive survey released **last summer**, 51 percent of respondents said Americans use their wireless phones **in a somewhat or very discourteous manner**. **Ironically**, 86 percent claim they, **personally**, **rarely** or **never** engage in discourteous phone use. (**discourteous** (adj): *formal* rude and lacking respect)

④ I learned the importance of America's engagement with the rest of the world, and I developed relationships with foreign leaders and an understanding of foreign cultures that come in **handy** today. I also learned how to keep focused while living in the eye of many storms.

⑤ Take time in your travels to explore this unique region and discover all that we have to offer. No matter what your pleasure, this area offers it all … shopping, dining, comfortable lodging, family attractions and entertainment, as well as a wide variety of events **sure** to please everyone. (if you **take your time** doing something, you do it quite slowly and do not hurry.)

Unit 21 Degree adverbs

GRAMMAR NOTES

Not all verbs, adjectives, etc. can be modified by degree adverbs. Degree applies only to gradable words, i.e. words whose meaning can be thought of in terms of a scale. There are two main kinds of gradable words: scale words and limit words.

Scale words indicate a relative position on a scale (e.g. *large, small*)

Limit words indicate the end-position of a scale (e.g. *black, white*)

(1) Degree with scale words (with adjective / verb scale words)

(a) indicating extreme position on the scale (*very* / (*very*) *much, a lot, a great deal*)

- He's *very* friendly. / I like her *very much.*
- It's a *very* tall building.

(b) intensifying the meaning slightly (*quite, rather, fairly, pretty* / *considerably, rather, quite, a lot*)

- She's still *quite* young. / I *quite* enjoy the job.
- She was *pretty* annoyed. / We talked *a lot* about old time.

(c) toning down or decreasing the effect of the scale word (*a bit, a little, slightly* / *a bit, a little, slightly*)

- She's *a bit* upset. / I've read *a bit* about it.
- The journey was *slightly* uncomfortable. / Prices have fallen *slightly.*
- It's *a little* surprising. / I know him *a little.*

(2) Degree with limit words

(a) adverbs indicating that the limit's words meaning is used to its fullest extent: *absolutely, altogether, completely, entirely, quite, totally, utterly,*

- I'm *absolutely* positive it's truth.
- I *completely* disagree with you.
- We were *utterly* powerless to defend ourselves.

(b) adverbs indicating a position near the limit of the scale: *almost, nearly, practically, virtually*

- Mr. Player was *almost* in tears.
- I've *nearly* finished my work.

GRAMMATICAL EXPLORATION IN CONTEXT

① About 60 percent of the drivers were undergraduate students, Lutz said. This number stays **pretty** stationary from year to year.
(**stationary** (adj): not moving. *Stationary cars in traffic jams cause a great deal of pollution.*)

② "I cried **a lot**, and I prayed **a lot**. Those who came to see us kept asking: 'When is he going to die?' But he's not dead," said Getruda.

③ Then at twilight in the beautiful Lake District of England, we found ourselves on the shores of Lake Ennerdale, where Bill asked me to marry him. I was **desperately** in love with him but **utterly** confused about my life. So I said, "No, not now." What I meant, "Give me time."
(**desperately**: very, very much: *I was desperately lonely. John desperately wanted to go to college.*)

④ I hate French fries. The French didn't even create them, so why do they lay claim to them? I'd **much prefer** they **be** called freedom fires or Aussie chips.
(**lay (make / stake) claim to**: say officially that you believe that something belongs to you. **Aussie**: adj. *informal* relating to Australia or its culture)

⑤ This product carries a 60 days unconditional, no-risk guarantee. If you are not **totally** satisfied, your purchase price will be refunded. No questions asked. There is also a one year warranty.
(**totally** (adv): completely. **no questions** (asked): (There is) no question about that: something is definitely true. **warranty** (n) = guarantee)

Unit 22 Position of adverbs

GRAMMAR NOTES

(1) Main positions for adverbs

There are three main positions for adverbs which modify a verb: end, front and mid position.

(a) **End** position: immediately after the verb or later in the clause
- They *played quietly* all day.
- We tried to *leave quietly*.

(b) **Front** position: before the subject
- *Finally he* could stand the noise no longer.
- The value of the yen has fallen. *As a result*, Japan faces a crisis.

(c) **Mid** position: between the subject and verb, immediately after *be* as a main verb, or after the first auxiliary verb
- The street lighting was so bad that *we almost missed* the turning.
- She *is usually* here by 10.00.
- They *would usually* come by car.

(2) More than one adverbial in end position

- She sang *perfectly in the town hall last night*. (manner/place/time)
- He drove *to the beach quickly this morning*. (place/manner/time)
- He was working *hard there then*. (manner/place/time)
- In the accident she was thrown *violently forwards*. (manner/place)
- We arrived *here on Saturday*. (place/time)
- They left at *3.00 with a great deal of noise*. (time/manner)
- We had dinner *in a revolving restaurant in Goldcoast*. (place/place)
- I'll call on you *at ten o'clock tomorrow*. (time/time)
- He got drunk *tonight within a very short time*. (time/time)
- He was arrested *last year at the customs desk of Bangkok international airport*. (time/place)

GRAMMATICAL EXPLORATION IN CONTEXT

① Babies **often** don't have much of an appetite when they're sick, so while food is optional – even for several days – it's essential that they drink enough to prevent dehydration. Fluids **also** help flush out germs.
(**flush out**: clean something using a lot of water)

② You can **also** let your child sleep in his stroller, slightly reclined, or in a car seat. "I've **actually** put the entire car seat in the crib," says Mary Lyon, author of The Frazzled Working Woman's Guide to Motherhood.
(**crib** (n): a small bed for a baby with tall sides that have bars. **frazzled** (adj): extremely tired)

③ "They're **mostly** sugar and water, but since sugar is the main ingredient in anti-nausea syrups – and my kids are **often** sick with vomiting – that's **probably** a good thing."
(**nausea** (n) : the feeling that you are going to vomit)

④ As children, my brothers and I spent **a lot of time at his duplex on Diamond Avenue in Scranton**, and each summer we spent **most of August at the cottage** he had built in 1921 **about twenty miles northwest of Scranton in the Pocono Mountains** overlooking Lake Winola.

⑤ Della essentially abandoned my mother when she was only three or four, leaving her alone all day for days on end **with meal tickets to use at a restaurant near their five-story walk-up apartment on Chicago's South Side.**

Unit 23 Comparisons

GRAMMAR NOTES

(1) Equatives

- Was the film *as funny as* his last one?
- Despite his disability, he tried to lead *as normal a life as* possible.
- It's *not as quiet a place* (or ··· *not such a quiet place*) *as* it used to be.

(2) Comparatives

(a) *more / less* + one-syllable adjectives

- I'd ironed my shirt it looked *more creased* than before. (past participle adjectives: *bored, creased, pleased, worn,* ···)
- I expected the film to be rather dull, but I couldn't have been *more wrong.* (*fun, real, right* and *wrong,* ···)
- Personally, I thought he was *more mad* than *brave.* (= ··· was*n't so much brave as mad*) (comparing two qualities)
- You might think it's dark here but it's *more dark / darker* in the cellar. (*clear, cold, dark, rough, soft, true,* ···) (to emphasize the comparison)

(b) *more / less* + two-syllable adjectives

(i) participle adjectives (e.g. *worried, boring*)

(ii) adjectives ending in *-ful* and *-less* (e.g. *careful. careless*); *afraid, alert, alike, alone, ashamed, aware*

(iii) some other adjectives: including *active, cautious, certain, complex, direct, eager, exact, formal, frequent, modern, special, recent.*

(3) *The* + comparatives

- *The higher* the wall, *the less* it works. (the U. S. – Mexican border)
- Of the two paintings, the one by Klee is *the more interesting.*
- She was looking all *the better for* her stay in hospital. (= because of ...)

(4) Other forms used to express comparison

- Mary is tall *for* a girl.
- John is tall *compared* to Joey.
- John's height *exceeds / surpasses* Mary's (height).
- Bill *out*played his opponents.
- The professor *over / under*rated his own worth.
- It happened *over* a hundred years ago.
- Bob's annual salary is *under* $20,000.

GRAMMATICAL EXPLORATION IN CONTEXT

① Researchers at the University of Rochester found that exposure to secondhand smoke makes children **twice as** likely to get cavities **as** those not exposed to cigarette fumes. "Nicotine enhances the growth in the mouth of bacteria that causes some cavities," says study author Michael Weitzman, MD. (**enhance** (n): to improve something. **cavity** (n): a hole in a tooth, caused by decay)

② Children under 3 are especially vulnerable: Their immune systems aren't yet fully developed, so they're **less** capable of fighting off illness. And when they do get sick, their symptoms can be **more** severe **than** those of older kids exposed to the same viruses or bacteria.

③ U.S. parents are **more worried** about the amount of time their kids spend watching television or meeting friends on Internet social networks **than** about sex or alcohol abuse, according to Common Sense Media, a San Francisco-based group that studies the impact of media on kids.

④ Diaper rash occurs because your infant's skin is in contact with urine and stool; therefore, **the drier and cleaner** you can keep him, **the less rashy** he should be.

⑤ **The highest** injury rate was observed among the 11-to-14-year-old group, which accounted for 43 percent of all injuries. Lower-extremity injuries were **the most common** type of injury among this group and older teens. **The next most-injured** segment was the 5-to-9-year-old group. In this group, head injuries accounted for **more than** half of all injuries. Teens aged 15 to 19 years old were slightly **less prone** to experiencing an accident **than** the youngest group.

Unit 24 Moods

GRAMMAR NOTES

(1) The term 'mood' is most usually applied to inflectional systems of the verb, as in the contrast between *indicative, subjunctive*, and *imperative*.

Indicative mood (*fact-mood*: statements and questions about facts)
- I'm thirsty.
- Unless you put on your coat, you'll catch a cold.

Imperative mood (*will-mood*: commands and instructions)
- Give me something to drink.
- You'd better put your coat on, or (else) you'll catch a cold.

Subjunctive mood (*thought-mood*: doubts, wishes, suggestions, requests, and non-facts with *that* or *if*)
- I wish I *had* something to drink.
- I *would* wear an overcoat if I *were* you; otherwise, you'll catch a cold.

(2) Because the subjunctive creates a rather formal tone, many people today tend to substitute the indicative mood in informal conversation.
- I *suggested* that he *should give up* golf. (BrE)
- I *suggested* that he *give up* golf. (AmE: subjunctive, more formal)
- I *suggested* that he *gives up* golf. (indicative, less formal)

(*demand, move, order, prefer, propose, recommend, request, require,* ⋯)
- She *insists* that he *take / took / takes* the eight o'clock train.
- Witnesses *insisted* that the accident *had taken* place on the crosswalk.
- The *requirement* was that every member *be /should be* good at English.
- The *suggestion* that he *be / should be / is* fired met with resistance.

(*insistence, order, proposal, request, recommendation, requirement,* ⋯)
- It is *essential* that everyone *attends / attend / should attend* the meeting. (*advisable, appropriate, crucial, imperative, important, necessary, preferable, right, urgent, vital,* ⋯)
- It is *strange* that he *should be / is* so late. (indicative, less formal)
- I am *concerned* that she *should think / thinks* I stole the money. (*amazed, anxious, concerned, disappointed, disappointed, embarrassing, frightening, shocked, surprised, surprising, upset, willing,* ⋯)

GRAMMATICAL EXPLORATION IN CONTEXT

① French officials **responded** brusquely today to an assertion by Secretary of State Colin L. Powell that France **would** be made to suffer for its opposition to the war in Iraq.

② On March 16, 1919, Washington College students presented a petition to the faculty **requesting** that student government **be** established on the campus and that an honor system **be** adopted. Though the faculty did not give formal permission for student government to be established until May 27 of the same year, it is generally **accepted** that March 16, 1919 **be** remembered as the date that the Washington College Student Government Association (SGA) was founded.

③ In April, officials from the United States, North Korea and China met in Beijing to review the situation. Since then, the administration **has insisted** that Japan and South Korea **be** allowed to take part in a second round, and said that Russia would be a welcome participant.

④ We face the strong possibility of another Korean War, with potentially devastating consequences, so the endangered multilateral talks in Beijing are of paramount importance. It is **vital** that some accommodation **be** reached between Pyongyang and Washington.

⑤ President Vladimir Putin said Thursday that tests of new Russian missiles this week were a response to US plans for missile defense sites and other forces in Europe, and **suggested** Washington **is** pursuing an imperialist policy that has triggered a new arms race.

Unit 25 Imperatives

GRAMMAR NOTES

(1) Forms of imperatives

- Open the door.
- Watch yourself!
- You be quiet! / You bring me a cup of coffee!
- Be on time!
- Don't you run. / Don't run.
- Don't you be late! / Don't be late!
- Never be late again!
- Let's go to the movies.
- Somebody open the door. / Mac, open the door. / Mac, you open the door.

(2) Functions of imperatives (in addition to commands)

- Help yourself. (offer)
- Close the door, please. (requests)
- Don't forget Mother's Day. (advice)
- Go left at the next corner. (direction)
- Do not pick the flowers. (prohibition)
- Come in. (invitation)
- Watch out! (warning)
- Have a great day! (wish)

(3) Politeness and the use of imperatives

Least polite	imperative(elliptical)	A glass of water.
(most direct)	imperative	Give me a glass of water.
	declarative	I want / need a glass of water.
	declarative	I'll have a glass of water.
	declarative	I'd like a glass of water.
	interrogative	Can you give me a glass of water?
Most polite	interrogative	Could you give me a glass of water?
(least direct)		

GRAMMATICAL EXPLORATION IN CONTEXT

① **Wait** until the bus comes to a complete stop and then board at the front door of the bus. Please **have** your exact fare, token, or pass ready to show the driver as you board the bus. **Remember** drivers cannot give change.

② Do you have a funny story about your dog / dogs behaving really badly? **Send** it to us in 300 words or less. The top two stories will be published in the October 16th Issue. Please **include** your dog's breed and age at the time of the incident.

③ If you hit a wayward shot that you think might endanger others, **shout** "fore!" loudly and without hesitation. **Do not be shy** – it is better to be safe than sorry. Also, **be certain** that the group ahead of you is out of range before you hit your shot. Again, **err** on the side of caution.

(**wayward** (adj): not controlled in the right way. **err on the side of sth**: to do more than is really necessary in order to avoid a particular situation, *We are erring on the side of caution and have closed the school*)

④ **Touch** your partner's belly often and **feel** your baby kicking. **Talk** to the baby so she can get used to the sound of your voice. **Listen** to classical music with your partner and **know** that your baby can hear and enjoy the music as well.

⑤ This medication comes as a tablet and a liquid. It is usually taken every 12 hours. **Take** this medication as prescribed. **Be** sure to follow instructions closely. **Do not** increase your dose or take this more often than directed. This medication is best taken with a full glass of water after a meal or snack. **Do not** chew or crush the tablet.

(**medication** (n): drugs that you take to treat or cure an illness.)

Unit 26 Real conditionals

GRAMMAR NOTES

(1) Three conditional structures

- If I *have* the money, I *will* take a vacation. (*real* conditional)
- If I *had* the money, I *would* take a vacation. (*unreal* past conditional)
- If I *had had* the money, I *would have taken* a vacation. (*unreal* past perfect conditional)

(2) Real conditionals suggest that the situation is or was true, or may have been or may become true.

(a) simple present

- If she *makes* a promise, she keeps it.
- If I *go* to Seoul, I'll travel by train.

  cf. If I *went* to Seoul, I*'d* travel by train.
- If you *leave* now, you'll be home in two hours.
- If you*'re* scared of spiders, don't go into the garden.
- I'll give you a ride if it *rains.*
- I'll lend Peter the money if he *needs* it.

(b) present perfect

- If you*'ve finished* your homework, you may / can go out and play.
- If you *haven't paid* the bill by Friday, we're taking the carpets back. (or if you *don't pay* …)

(c) simple past

- If I *made* the wrong decision then I apologize.
- If the flight *was* on time, he should have arrived in Pusan early this morning.

  cf. If the flight *had been* on time, he *would have arrived* in Pusan early this evening.
- If that *was* Mary, why didn't she stop and say hello?

(d) past perfect

- If he *hadn't left* any message when you called, he probably intends to be back before you leave.

GRAMMATICAL EXPLORATION IN CONTEXT

① **If** Pennsylvania **does** not change the legal blood alcohol content from 0.10 to 0.08 percent by 2004, it **will** face federal funding cuts.

② **If** you**'ve never had** an account with Verizon, you**'ll** be sent a credit application to complete. There is a $40 charge per line when you add a new connection or move your phone service from one address to another.

③ Speaker after speaker **warned** that young doctors were leaving Pennsylvania and that patients **would** lose access to health care **if** mushrooming malpractice premiums **were** not curbed. (**mushroom** (v): to increase or develop very quickly. **curb** (v): to control or limit something that is harmful)

④ Ahmadi said militants were still demanding the release of 23 Taliban prisoners but said the government hadn't signaled it was willing to do that. "**If** the government **won't accept** these conditions, then it's difficult for the Taliban to provide security for these 23 South Korean hostages, to provide health facilities and food," Ahmadi told The Associated Press by satellite phone. "The Taliban won't have any option but to kill the hostages." (**Ahmadi**: a Taliban spokesman)

⑤ But, chocolate does have some bad effects. It contains a lot of fats and sugar, so **if** people **eat** too much, they can develop or worsen conditions such as hardening of the arteries or diabetes. Doctors and dentists have been telling patients for a long time that **if** their fat and sugar intake **were** lower, they **would** be healthier. Such warnings do not do much to inhibit chocoholics. Says one chocoholic, "Quite frankly, **if** I **had** a day without chocolate, it **would** be like a day without sunshine."

Unit 27 Unreal Conditionals

GRAMMAR NOTES

Unreal conditionals suggest that the situation is imaginary or untrue.

(1) Subjunctive present
- I require that term papers *be* turned in on time.
- The job demands that employees *be* in good physical condition.
- God *be* with you.

(2) Subjunctive past
- I *would lend* Peter the money if he *needed* it.
- If my grandfather *was / were* still alive, he *would* be a hundred today.
- If you *were driving* from London to Glasgow, which way *would* you go?
- What *would* you do if you *won* the lottery?
- If the technology *were to* become available, we *would* be able to expand the business.
- If I *knew* they were honest, I*'d* gladly lend them the money. (*If I were to know….) (We don't usually *if … were to* pattern with stative verbs such as *belong, doubt, enjoy, know, like, remember, understand,* …)

(3) Subjunctive past perfect and mixed
- I *would have lent* Peter the money if he *had needed* it.
- If you *had started* out earlier, you *wouldn't have been* so late.
- If the doctor *had been* called earlier, she *would* still be alive today.
- You *would* know the answer if you *had read* the book.
- If you really *liked* Jane, you *wouldn't have said* that.
- If Bob *wasn't* so lazy, he *would have passed* the exam easily.

(4) Idiomatic phrases and other special uses
- *Isn't it time* the children *went* to bed?
- "I *wish* I *could* live in this country as an ordinary Iraqi civilian," he said.
- *If only* I were a little younger! (= I do *wish* I were …)
- I should have failed *had it not been for your help.*
- Much of what happened in New Orleans *might have been avoided.*
- Humans are social animals which *would* be extinct if they *did* not look after each other.

GRAMMATICAL EXPLORATION IN CONTEXT 

① If golf **was** an exact science you **would** be able to leave yourself with your ideal distance pitch shot every time – and you **would** never hit a bad shot. But golf is not like that, and inevitably you have to play pitch shots from a variety of distances during a normal round.

② She softened hurts, mediated quarrels and won over many political opponents. Johnson often said his political ascent **would have been** inconceivable **without** his wife's devotion and forbearance. Others shared that belief.

③ The evolution of this important invention did not occur overnight. How fortunate we are that lightweight cans and easy-to-use can openers were invented; **otherwise**, **we would not have** the convenience and variety in foods that we have.

④ One mom told me how a cellphone helped her 14-year-old cheat. The girl and her friends used text messaging – transmitting things like "1C" and "2D" – to share answers on a multiple-choice test. **A few years ago**, it **would have been** harder to cheat that way.

⑤ My friend. "Tom," recently died from a heart attack. He was only 53 years old. Besides the grief, everyone experienced additional anguish because Tom didn't leave a will. The worst thing for me was to find out that the day after his death, his best friend had Tom's two little dogs put to sleep. The vet was told that that's what Tom wanted. I believe otherwise, but unfortunately, there was no document saying so. **Had Tom made** it clear, in writing, those cute little dogs **would be** alive today and living with his brother, who **would have been** happy to take them.

Unit 28 *Should, ought to, shall*

GRAMMAR NOTES

(1) *Should, ought to*

(a) obligation (talking about what is right, sensible, or correct)
- I *should / ought to* phone my parents tonight. ('but I probably won't have time')
  cf. I *must* phone my parents tonight. ('They'll be worrying about me.')
- They *should have been finished* yesterday.

(b) probability
- I mailed the letter today, so they *should* receive it by Monday.
- She's been studying hard for the exam, so she *should* pass.
- There *shouldn't / oughtn't to* be any difficulties.
- You *should have received* the report by now.
- By the time you get home I *should* (*will / may*) have cleaned the house from top to bottom.

(c) advice
- The diet *should* be maintained unchanged for about a year.
- You've been smoking too much lately. You *should* smoke less.
- Caution: Honey *should* not be used in foods for infants under one year of age.
- I *shouldn't / wouldn't* worry about it *if I were you.* (* ought not to …)

(d) surprise
- It surprises me that he *should* worry about it.
- I'm making these plans and who *should* I meet but this blonde guy.

(2) *Shall*

- We *shall* hear the results of the election within a week. (prediction)
- *Shall we* dance? (suggestion)
- *Shall I* help you with your luggage? (offer)
- The Court *shall* have authority to demand the presence of witness.
- The Society's nominating committee *shall* nominate one person for the office of President. (regulation, rule – very formal)

GRAMMATICAL EXPLORATION IN CONTEXT 

① Cell phones can be helpful in an emergency. But they can also be a distraction when you are driving. You **should** also avoid eating, reading or applying make-up when you're behind the heel.
(**apply**: to put a layer of something such as a paint onto a surface)

② One of General Hoar's most important military assessments, in fact, may have been the one he conveyed to Dr. Dean in a telephone conversation last spring. The retired general told the candidate that the administration of George W. Bush would have enormous difficulty stabilizing Iraq and that Dr. Dean **should** "stay on message" on Iraq.

③ With one birdie and one bogey today, Wie shot an even-par 71, six strokes off the lead. Tied for 51st place, she was not happy.
"I think I played pretty bad," she said softly outside the scorer's tent. "I think I could've made a lot of birdies and I **should have**. I wanted to shoot lower, like three or four under, because I wanted to be up on the leader board. I'm kind of bummed out because I wanted to do better."

④ "This tragedy is especially heartbreaking, first because the victims were so young," Daley said. "Secondly, because it was a disaster that absolutely **should never have happened**."

⑤ No person **shall** have in possession a deer, bear or turkey that he himself or she herself did not kill unless it has a tag bearing the name, address, telephone number, license and permit number of the person who killed the deer, bear or turkey. (New Jersey General Hunting Regulations)

Unit 29 *Will, would, used to*

GRAMMAR NOTES

(1) Will, would

(a) prediction

- Temperatures tomorrow *will* be much the same as today.
- Six-country talks *will* be held later this month to discuss eliminating North Korea's nuclear-weapons program.
- There*'ll* be trouble, unless this is finished by tomorrow.

(b) certainty

- You *will* know that John and Sheila are engaged.
- As you *will* all probably already know, election day is next week.
- As you *will have noticed*, he has cut off his beard. (past certainty)
- We *will have gone* to bed by the time you arrive.
- They*'ll* have got home by now, won't they?
- I *would have been* happy to see him, but I didn't have time.

(c) volition

- The manager said he *would* phone me after lunch. (volition)
- I shall be glad if he *will* come. (willingness)
- If you *won't* tell him the truth, I *will*. (refusal)
- If you *will* do it at all, do it well. (insistence)

(d) request, advice, or suggestion

- *Would* you please tell me your phone number? (tentative request)
- I*'d* be careful if I were you.
- It *would* be wise to discuss this with your bank manager.

(2) Will, would, used to: present or past habit

- She*'ll* sit on the floor quietly all day.
- They*'ll* happily spend the whole day playing computer games.
- As a child, I hated my strict bedtime, but my mom *would* never budge.
- Tim *would / used to* visit his parents every other weekend.
- On winter evenings we*'d* all sit around the fire.
- I *used to* smoke heavily when I was at university.
- In his youth, Leo *used to* be thin.
- They *used to* wear a size 6, but she doesn't anymore.
- I *used to* enjoy gardening, but I don't have time for it now.

GRAMMATICAL EXPLORATION IN CONTEXT 

① BEIJING – Amid high tensions and low expectations, representatives of six nations **will** gather in China's capital Wednesday for three days of talks aimed at easing the nuclear standoff with North Korea.

② In the Philippines, moviegoers who purchase any two tickets to watch *the Pirates of the Caribbean: At World's End* at any SM cinema nationwide from May 23 to June 5, **will** be eligible to win a trip for two to Singapore. The winner **will** be awarded round-trip air tickets, hotel accommodations and vouchers to Singapore's attractions and experiences.

③ During my pregnancy our cat **would** lie on my growing belly and purr herself to sleep while our baby kicked. When the cat felt a kick, he **would** tap my stomach with his tail and the baby **would** kick back. This **would** go on for minutes as just lay there, amused.

④ I **used to** call my 10-year-old cat, Po Patty, "my baby girl." But now I have a daughter, and while Po's needs **used to** come first, now it's Grace's, followed by my own (and, of course, my husband's).

⑤ Those who missed the first U.S Women's Amateur Championship at Philadelphia Country Club **would have experienced** a long wait for the next one, but it is finally almost here. (**would (will) have experienced**: past certainty)

Unit 30 *May, might, can, could*

GRAMMAR NOTES

(1) Possibility

- There *may* be an easier way of solving the problem
- The injury *may / might / could* (*can) *have caused* brain damage.
- I thought I saw Tom in town, but I *may / might / could* have been wrong.
- By next Friday I *may / might / could have completed* the report.
  cf. The plan *might / could* easily *have gone* wrong, but in fact it was a great success.
- A: *Can* it be true? B: Yes, it *may / might / could.* (* can)
- *Can* (*may) he be working? (= Is it possible that he is working?)
- A: *Can / Could* they have missed the train?
  B: Yes, they *may / might / could* …
- We *could* stay with Jim in Oslo. (= it's *possible*; if he's there)
- Even expert drivers *can* (*may/*might/*could) make mistakes. (general)
- You *can* travel from London to New York in under 6 hours these days.
- Tickets *can* be bought form the Tourist Information Center.

(2) Permission

- *May* I use your phone? (formal)
- Visitors *may* use the swimming pool between 5:30 and 7:30 p.m.
- You *may* take a short break now.
- A: *Can* I hold the baby? B: Yes, you *can.* (informal)

(3) Offer or request

- *May / Can / Could* I help you with those bags?
- *Can* you tell me where Mr. Lawson's office is?
- (*May* I see your) ticket, please?

(4) Wish

- *May* you / he rest in peace.
- God *bless* you and your baby.
- (*May*) God bless you.

(5) Impossibility

- You *can't* be serious, Mrs. Lorimer?
- He wasn't there at the time. It *can't / couldn't* have been his fault.
- There *can / could hardly* be any doubt that he was guilty.

GRAMMATICAL EXPLORATION IN CONTEXT

① If you hold a valid foreign driver's license with a valid International Driving Permit you **may** drive up to one year in Pennsylvania before obtaining a PA Driver's License.

② At the end of the meeting, the official said, Mr. Bush gave the go-ahead to the commanders to begin the war at the time they judged best, saying, "For the peace of the world and benefit and freedom of the Iraqi people, I hereby give the order to execute Operation Iraqi Freedom. **May** God Bless the troops." General Franks replied, "**May** God bless America," and exchanged salutes with the president, who then left the room.
(**give / get the go-ahead**: to give / get the permission to do something.)

③ A busy schedule, stress, anxiety, lack of exercise, and insufficient fluid intake **can** all have adverse effects on the body's normal bowel rhythm. Low fiber intake and a poorly balanced diet **can** aggravate the situation, leading to constipation. More than the physical discomfort, constipation **can** result to sickness and diseases.

④ People weighing 30 or more pounds too much **could** lose about seven years from their lives. And carrying even 10 to 30 extra pounds **could** shorten a person's life span by about three years, a study reports today.

⑤ Electricity generation stations throughout the United States are interconnected in a system called power grids. This allows electricity generated in one state to be sent to users in another state. It also allows distant power generation stations to provide electricity for cities and towns whose power generators **may have failed** or **been destroyed** by some accident or sabotage.

Unit 31 *Can, could, be able to, be allowed to*

GRAMMAR NOTES

(1) Ability: *can* vs. *be able to*

We sometimes use *be able to* instead of *can* and *could* to talk about ability. However, we avoid *be able to* (a) when we talk about something that is happening as we speak (b) before passives (c) when the meaning is 'know how to':

- Watch this, Mom; I *can* stand on one leg.
- This bicycle *can* be assembled by anyone, with just a screwdriver.
- *Can* you cook?

(2) Past ability: *could* vs. *was / were able to*

If we talk about a specific achievement, rather than a general ability in the past, we usually use *be able to* rather than *could*: However, *could* is usually more natural (a) in negative sentences, (b) with verbs of senses (*feel, hear, see, smell, taste,*…) and with verbs of 'thinking' (*believe, decide, remember, understand,*…) (c) after the phrases *the only thing / place / time,* and after *all* when it means 'the only thing', (d) to suggest that something almost didn't happen, particularly with *almost, hardly, just, nearly*:

- Mira's mother *could / was able to* speak Japanese and English.
- The fire spread through the building very quickly, but everyone *was able to / * could* escape.
- We tried hard but we *couldn't* persuade them to come with us.
- I *could* remember the crash, but nothing after that.
- All we *could* do was sit and wait. (= We couldn't do anything more.)
- I *could* nearly touch the ceiling.

(3) Past permission: *could* vs. *was / were allowed to*

- Anyone *was allowed to / could* fish in the lake when the council owned it. (general)
- Although he didn't have the necessary papers, he *was allowed to / * could* enter the country. (specific)
- We *couldn't / weren't allowed to* open the presents until Christmas morning. (negative)

GRAMMATICAL EXPLORATION IN CONTEXT

① We have enjoyed having you with us and hope that life will treat you well in the future. I will need a forwarding address at the rental office and you **can** use the enclosed one to change your address with the United States Mail.

② While it is forecast that the intensity of the hurricane will be diminished by the time it reaches the commonwealth on Thursday afternoon, the expected strong winds and several inches of rain on already-saturated areas **could** cause some problems, including power outages and flooding.

③ "Yesterday evening the Iraqi forces **were able to** take control of Falluja hospital to defeat the terrorists and armed groups so the citizens of Falluja will get help," he said.

④ Jacobs **could have won** with a bogey on the final hole, although he achieved a fine par from the rough, but just a few holes before that, a half dozen players were one or two under par.

⑤ At the time the Student Government Association was formed, only male students **were allowed to** participate. It wasn't until 1950s that the student body came to its senses and both men and women **were allowed to** participate together.

Unit 32 *Must, have to, have got to*

GRAMMAR NOTES

(1) Obligation

Must and *have* (*got*) *to* + infinitive both express obligation, but some English speakers feel a difference between them. For such speakers, *must* involves the speaker's authority, while *have* (*got*) *to* may involve some other authority than the speaker – e. g. official regulations. With a first person subject, *must* expresses my authority over myself, e.g. my sense of duty.

- You *must* / You *will have to* be back by 2 o'clock. (I want you to do some cleaning).
- I *must* phone my parents tonight. (They'll be worrying about me.)
- 'You *must* go.' → She said that they *must* / *had to* go.
- If you went abroad, you *would have to* earn your own living. (' … would be obliged to …')
- I*'ve got to* finish this essay by tomorrow. (informal)
- Why *have* you *got to* work so hard?
- You can tell me if you want but you *don't have to* tell me.
  cf. You must keep it a secret. You *mustn't* tell anyone.

(2) Certainty

- You're having a baby! You *must* be very happy.
- There *must* have been some misunderstanding. (past certainty)
- I think she *must have sensed* there was something wrong.
- "He *must have told* her." "No, surely he can't have done."
- You *have to* be joking! (= You*'ve got to* be joking)

(3) Strong advice or recommendation

- You *must* stop smoking or you'll die.
- It's half past two. I think we *had better* go home. (or we *should* / *ought to* …)
- (You'd)*Better* not say too much aloud.
- The party was great. You *should* / **had better have come*. Why didn't you? (past advice)
- You *should* / *ought to have caught* a later train. (*You *had better* have caught …)

GRAMMATICAL EXPLORATION IN CONTEXT

① Only one antlered deer may be taken per season statewide, regardless of the number of special season permits in possession. To be legal, all deer harvested **must** be registered at an official deer check station and have a metal possession seal affixed to the deer.

② Match play's a lot more different than stroke play. In stroke play you can go ahead and do your own thing, but in match play you'**ve got to** play against somebody else's ball and you **have to** be sure you don't make a big mistake.

③ Throughout the exercise, use exactly the same, standard chip shot technique. You **do not have to** change your swing each time you change club; instead, the different lofts on the clubs will produce shots of a different nature. Always pay close attention to the ball's height, carry, spin, and roll. Then when you are on the course, you will be able to select the most appropriate club for every chip.

④ The top players are all athletes now, but the new equipment **has to** take a lot of the credit as well. It wasn't so long ago that the driver was considered to be one of the hardest clubs in the bag to hit. Today it's one of the friendliest clubs – for golfers of all levels. You'**ve got to** thank companies like Callaway Golf for making golf more fun for everybody, not just Tour players.

⑤ If you like the outdoors and would like to learn more about conserving our forests, wildlife, and water, Penn State's one-week program for high school students just might be for you. To attend CLS (Conservation Leadership School) 2003, you should have a real interest in conservation and the environment. You **must** be 15 to 18 years old and **must have completed** ninth grade.

Unit 33 Sentence structures

GRAMMAR NOTES

(1) Basic types of sentence structures

- It(S) is snowing(V).
- My parents(S) are living(V) in Chicago(A).
- Your dinner(S) seems(V) ready(C).
- We(S) have finished(V) our work(O).
- I(S) must send(V) my parents(O) an anniversary card(O).
- Most students(S) have found(V) her(O) reasonably helpful(C).
- You(S) can put(V) the dish(O) on the table(A).

(2) Complementation: obligatory or optional

(a) The elements O, C, and A are obligatory elements of sentence structure in that they are required for the complementation of the verb. The same verb (sometimes in somewhat different senses) may enter into different structures.

- I have *eaten*. – I have *eaten* lunch.
- It *smells*. – It smells *sweet*.
- He *felt* a fool. – He *felt* a material.
- I *made* some sandwiches. – I *made* them some sandwiches.
- The children are *growing*. – The children are *growing* carrots. – The children are *growing* hungry.

(b) Adverbials are optional elements in sentence structure. However, some elements that convey the same information as adverbials are obligatory. The most common verb in the SVA structure is *be*, and adverbial complements typically refer to space or other meanings.

- The protestors were *outside the White House*.
- The nearest inhabitants are *a five-day mule trip away*.
- The city lies *225 miles north of Guatemala City*.
- George is getting *into his wife's car*.
- This roads goes *to Newark*.
- Their work is *in the early stage*.
- The show will last *for three hours*.
- The children were *with their mother*.
- These letters are *for Cindy*.

GRAMMATICAL EXPLORATION IN CONTEXT

① My doctor recommended Glucerna SR. Now I have the energy to play basketball with my son and travel long distances as part of my work. My eyesight has even improved! I feel better knowing I can live a normal life with my blood sugar under control.

② France, Germany and Russia all have **argued** that the inspectors **be** given more time to determine whether Iraq has weapons of mass destruction or programs to build them. And on Friday, more than 120 congressional Democrats **sent** President Bush a letter urging him to give the inspection process more time.

③ Researchers at the Henry Ford Healthcare System in Detroit **found** that infants who live with at least two dogs or cats (or one of each) in their first year of life **are** half as likely to develop allergies later in childhood (by the time they are 6 or 7) than those who live with no pets.

④ An enriched whitening lotion, the Sekkisei Lotion Excellent is an intensive toner that provides moisturizing, anti-aging and brightening benefits. Packed with Oriental herbal extracts and antioxidants, I **liked that** it easily absorbed on my skin leaving it deeply moisturized and firm.

⑤ Expensive cellphones are disappearing around the world every minute – snatched out of hands, picked from pockets, forgotten in taxis. But now, for the amateur detectives among us, there is software that, for $8, can tell you who stole your phone and help you hunt them down.

Until recently, **all you could do was ensure that** no one else used the phone by reporting its serial number and blocking it, either through your operator or a site like www.immobilise.com.

Unit 34 Subject-verb agreement

GRAMMAR NOTES

(1) Agreement of number

- Many books on the best-seller list *have* little literary value.
- The president, along with many senators, *opposes* the bill.
- Carla is *one of the employees* who always *work* late.
- Sam is *the only one of the* employees who always *works* overtime.

(2) Agreement with coordinated subjects

- Law and order *is* considered important in this election.
- Drinking and driving *remains* a major cause of highway fatalities.
- Monday and Tuesday *are* very busy for me.
- A backpack, a canteen, and a rifle *were* issued to each recruit.
- Two boxes of paper *were* delivered to our school.
- Two tablespoons of cooking oil *go* into the cake recipe.
- Neither my roommate nor *my neighbors like* my loud music.
- Either two onions or *a clove of garlic is* necessary for this recipe.
- A passenger, as well as the driver, *was* injured in the accident.

(3) Indefinite expressions: *any, no, none / neither, either*

- *None* of us *wants* to be killed young. (grammatical – written, formal)
- None of *us want* to be killed young. (notional – spoken, informal)
- I sent cards to Avis and Mary but neither of them *has / have* replied.
- In fact, I doubt if either of them *is / are* coming.

(4) *~body, ~one → they* (informal)

- Has *anybody* brought *their* camera?
- *Anybody* with any sense would have read the play in translation, wouldn't *they*?
- *Everyone* thinks *he* has the answer. (formal – traditional)
- *Everyone* thinks *they* have the answer. ('unisex' they – even in current written English)

(5) Group noun

- A committee *has* been set up so that in the future *it* will discuss such topics in advance. (grammatical agreement)
- The committee *believe* it is essential that *their* proposal should be adopted as soon as possible. (notional agreement)

GRAMMATICAL EXPLORATION IN CONTEXT

① Just a quick note to let you know that the following item that you have on your wish list at The Golf Warehouse **has** just been reduced in price.
(**wish list:** informal all the things that you would like to be given or would like to happen.)

② Reading to kids, extra hugs and kisses – anything that makes your child feel cared for – **is** the best medicine. Before you know it, your baby feel like his usual, adorable self.

③ Despite the desire to make changes, more than a year **has passed** since state leaders acknowledged severe problems in New York's adult homes for the mentally ill.

④ Some experts say that infancy **is** an ideal time to introduce a foreign language because the areas of the brain that **are** necessary for speech development **are** still being formed. Others say that it's better to wait until 2 or 3 years of age, when the child has a better understanding of English.

⑤ You might be surprised to learn that most key vitamins your child needs to grow up strong and healthy **aren't** stored in the body. But you can help replenish them every day, with Flintstones Complete. Taking a Flintstones each day **helps** ensure your child gets 100% of the daily value of 12 essential vitamins and minerals. They're the pediatricians' #1 choice. (**replenish** (v): to make something full or complete again)

Unit 35 Light verbs

GRAMMAR NOTES

Connected with the principle of end-weight in English is the feeling that the predicate of a clause should be longer or grammatically more complex than the subject. This helps to explain why we tend to avoid predicates consisting of just a single intransitive verb. Instead of saying *Mary sang*, many would probably prefer to say *Mary sang a song*, filling the object position with a noun phrase which adds little information but helps to give more weight to the predicate. For such a purpose English often uses a general verb (such as ***make, have, take, give, go*** and ***do***) followed by an abstract noun phrase.

Light verb constructions can be paraphrased to some extent by a single verb. The single-verb, intransitive paraphrases, however, lack a semantic dimension shared by the transitive sentences, light verb constructions; the transitive version suggested that the event is *time-bounded*, that it has a clear-cut beginning and end. *Michael had a smoke* suggests one cigarette, while *Michael smoked* does not. This is underscored by the fact that we can easily say *Pete and Lynn chatted for hours,* but *?? Pete and Lynn had a chat for hours* is odd.

- He just *made* his second big *mistake.* (**single time-bounded event**)
- He did not say what *progress* Washington hopes to *make.*
- She's *having a swim.*
- Sue *had* (*took*) *a look at* the book.
- He's *taking a bath.* / They *took a rest.*
- We're going to *do some climbing* in the Pyrenees.
- Excessive drinking will *do* you a lot of *harm.*
- Every morning, he *goes jogging* with his wife.
- On hot days the kids would *go swimming* in the river.
- I *gave* the door *a* couple of hard *kick.*
- She *gave* me *a wink.*
- I *paid* her *a visit.* cf. I *had a visit* from a stranger.
- He is a *good swimmer.* (= He swims well)
- He is a *frequent visitor* to the library.

GRAMMATICAL EXPLORATION IN CONTEXT

① Just before it disintegrated, the space shuttle Columbia experienced an abnormal rise in temperature and air resistance that forced the craft's automatic pilot to **make rapid changes** to its flight path – possible evidence that some heat-protection tiles were missing or damaged, NASA officials said yesterday. (**disintegrate** (v): to be completely destroyed by breaking into lots of very small pieces, for example, as the result of an explosion)

② Got a minute? Because now that's all it takes to manage your Verizon bill online, day or night. With just a couple of clicks, you can pay bill or view past statements in detail. You can even stay awhile and **take a look at** everything else Verizon offers you. (**statement** (n): an official document that lists the amount of money that have been put in or taken out of an bank account)

③ William R. McDonagh, President of McDonagh Chrysler Jeep located on Route 18, has just announced plans to **have a** $99 used car and truck **sale** this Saturday, September 20, 2003, between 9am and 2pm at his dealership. (**dealership** (n): a business that sells the products of a particular company, especially car)

④ He estimates he's regained about 75 percent of his physical movement. "I'm in the weight room three days a week and I **do conditioning** two days a week," he said. "It's a constant battle. Hopefully, one day I'll be fully recovered."

⑤ Thanksgiving is observed on the fourth Thursday in November. Incidentally, President Franklin Roosevelt tried to change the date of Thanksgiving to the third Thursday in November, in part to extend the holiday shopping season by one week and **give a boost** to the economy during the Great Depression. (**incidentally**: by the way)

Unit 36 Phrasal verbs

GRAMMAR NOTES

A phrasal verb is a verb formed from two (sometimes three) parts: a verb and an adverb or preposition. Most are formed from a small number of common verbs (such as get, go, come, put and set) and a small number of adverbs (*up, out, on, in, off, down,* ···) and prepositions (*to, with, for, in, on, into, about, of, at,* ···). These adverbs and prepositions are often called particles. There are five main types of phrasal verbs:

(1) Types of phrasal verbs

(a) intransitive verbs:

- You're driving too fast – you ought to *slow down.*

(b) transitive verbs whose object can come in two positions – after the verb or after the particle. If the object is a pronoun, however, it must come between the verb and the particle.

- I think I'll *put* my jacket *on* / I think I'll *put on* my jacket.
- I think I'll *put* it *on.* (* I think I'll *put on* it.)

(c) transitive verbs whose object must come between the verb and the particle.

- Its high quality designs *set* the company *apart* from its rivals.

(d) transitive verbs whose object must come after the particle.

- The baby takes after his mother.
- Why do you *put up with* the way he treats you?

(e) verbs with two objects – one after the verb, the other after the particle.

- They *put* their success *down to* a good planning.

(2) Passives with phrasal verbs

When some transitive phrasal verbs appear in the passive, nothing comes between the verb and the particle.

- Terrorists *blew up* the bridge / *blew* the bridge *up.*
  → The bridge was *blown up* by terrorists.
- *Turn* the lights *off* / *turn off* the lights before you leave.
  → Make sure the lights are *turned off* before you leave.
- It's time they *did away with* these silly rules.
  → It's time these silly rules were *done away with.*

GRAMMATICAL EXPLORATION IN CONTEXT

① You can choose from a tasty variety of pies including apple, cherry, strawberry rhubarb and more. **Stop in** and **pick up** one of these home-made delights today!

② Four young British citizens of Pakistani origin appear to have **carried out** last week's bombings of the London transit system, **blowing** themselves **up** along with their victims in what would be the first suicide attacks in Western Europe, British police said Tuesday. (**blow up**: to explode)

③ The Transportation Security Administration said American Flight 136 from Los Angeles to London made an emergency landing at JFK Airport around 4 a.m. The decision to divert was made after a flight attendant became suspicious about the behavior of one of the passengers, the airline said in a statement. American Airlines said the passenger has been **handed over to** the FBI. It offered no further details.

④ Todase, the physician, has become skilled at pumping the stomachs of the local farmers, but their survival **depends** largely **on** how close they live to the hospital. Farmers in remote areas usually **succumb to** the poison before the treatment can begin.

⑤ King Gyanendra of Nepal, who imposed absolute rule on his country 14 months ago, is getting isolated both domestically and internationally, and his options are fast **running out**. Gyanendra tried to reverse historical processes by **rolling back** the constitutional monarchy that **came about** after the success of the pro-democracy movement in 1990. But people, having tasted democratic rights, don't **give up on** them so easily. Gyanendra's fate has been sealed by the understanding arrived at between the seven-party alliance and the Maoist rebels, and a Nepali republic looks conceivable now.

Unit 37 *So* and *do so*

GRAMMAR NOTES

(1) *So, not, not … so*

We can use *so* instead of repeating an adjective, adverb, or a whole clause:
- The workers were *angry* and they had every right to be *so*.
- John took the work *seriously* and Petra perhaps even more *so*.
- *Bob's giving us a lift*. At least I presume *so*.

(a) *so* is a substitute for *that*-clauses after *'thinking verbs'* (*be afraid, appear, seem, assume, believe, expect, guess, hope, imagine, presume, say, suppose, suspect, think,* …).
(b) *not* replaces *so* in negative clauses with *be afraid, assume, guess, hope, presume, suspect,* … .
(c) either *not* or *not* … *so* with *appear, seem, suppose,* …
(d) and with verbs taking transferred negation (*believe, expect, imagine, suppose, think,* …), it is more natural to use *not*… *so*.
- "Has Ivan gone home?" "I think *so*."
- "You'd better do it yourself. Brian won't help." "No, I guess *not*."
- "Will we need to show our passports at the border?" "I do*n't* think *so*."

(2) *Do so, do it, do that*

Do so is most often used in formal spoken and written English. In informal English we can use *do it* or *do that* instead. We can use *do so* instead of verbs that describe *action*, but we avoid *do so* with verbs that describe *states* and *habitual actions*.
- If you want me to *invite Kim,* I will *do so*.
- I didn't need to *water the flowers*; I could see that Anne had already *done so / done it / done that*.
- They say he *sleeps in his shoes and socks*. Why ever does he *do that*?
- 'Do you think John already *knows*?' 'I think everybody *does*.'
- I don't have time to *go swimming* every day, but I *usually do*.
- He *earned* a lot more than I *did*.

GRAMMATICAL EXPLORATION IN CONTEXT

① My mother is giving my wife a card on Father's Day? Doesn't anybody understand the irony here? I **guess not**.

② Are you paying too much for life insurance? Find out how you can save up to 70%. At AccuQuote, we help you compare the price, features, and financial strength of hundreds of life insurance products. By **doing so**, our clients typically save up to 70%.

③ But they said an eruption is God's will and only prayer, not the government, can protect them. Officials, careful not to discount the importance of these beliefs, struggle to move villagers to safety. So far, only a few hundred people, mostly old women and young children, have been evacuated. And they **did so** reluctantly.

④ Ohio State football coach Jim Tressel said that Penn State made the plays in the game and that made the difference. "Penn State did a great job of making plays. I thought our kids hung in there and fought hard," Tressel said. "Our players tried to make plays of their own and had a chance at the end of the game that could have made a difference. And we didn't **do that**."

⑤ Bush went on to say that he had not spent "a lot of time" talking with people in his administration about court testimony in the Libby case. But he added: "I'm aware of the fact that perhaps somebody in the administration did disclose the name of that person, and I've often thought about what would have happened had that person come forth and said, 'I **did it**.' Would we have had this, you know, endless hours of investigation and a lot of money being spent on this matter?"

Unit 38 Prepositions after verbs

GRAMMAR NOTES

All prepositional verbs take a prepositional object, i.e. the noun phrases occurring after the preposition. There are two major structural patterns for prepositional verbs:

(1) Pattern 1: NP + verb + preposition + NP

- *Think about* what I've told you.
- I've never even *thought about* it.
- Doesn't he *look like* Mark?
- He's always reluctant to *ask for* anyone's help.
- Joe *competes with / against* his older brother too much.
- I spent the morning *dealing with* my emails.
- He finished the drink quickly and *asked for* another.
- He got angry when they *asked* (*inquired*) *after* this private life.
- Jan *cared for* her disabled mother until her death last year.
- Would you *care for* a cup of coffee?
- You should *provide for* your old age now.

(**at**: *glance, look, smile, stare,* **to**: *amount, attend, belong, conform, contribute, happen, lead, listen, object, occur, refer, resort, speak, talk,* **for**: *account, allow, go, hope, look, pay, qualify, wait / agree on/with/to, apologize for/to, appeal for /to, apply for/to, bring back, consist of, differ from, get over, get through, go through, insist on, leave out, look into, run into, succeed in/to, suffer from/with, sympathize with, turn down,* …)

(2) Pattern 2: NP + verb + NP + preposition + NP

- I think the media is falsely *accused of* a lot of things.
  cf. People falsely *accuse* the media *of* a lot of things.
- He *said* farewell *to* us on this very spot.
- Prices are *based on* two people sharing a room.
- The Red Cross *provided* us *with* blankets.

(*be applied to, be associated with, be charged with, be composed of, be considered as, be derived from, fill ~with, be included in, be involved in, be known as, be made of, be regarded as, be related to,* …)

GRAMMATICAL EXPLORATION IN CONTEXT

① At address, Annika **focuses** primarily **on** good balance and comfort, with her whole body relaxed and tension-free.

② Under pressure from world leaders, including British Prime Minister Tony Blair, Bush has **signed off on** a deal with the British to forgive billions of dollars African nations **owe to** international organizations such as the World Bank, the officials said yesterday. World leaders appear likely to approve a debt forgiveness plan next month in Scotland, at an economic summit of the seven richest nations and Russia, known as the Group of Eight.
(**sign off on**: *AmE informal* (sign off on sth) to officially agree to something. **forgive** (v): if a country or bank *forgives a debt*, they decide that the debt does not have to be paid back)

③ Those who drive their own vehicles to the summit are **treated to** an audio tour on cassette or CD that shares classic tales about the road's history, its geography and legends. Also included is the world famous "THE CAR CLIMBED MT. WASHINGTON" bumper sticker!

④ Iran declared Tuesday that it would soon resume some of the nuclear activities it had suspended during negotiations with Europe, and it used a conference here to **accuse** the United States and other nations **of** using the fear of nuclear weapons proliferation to deny peaceful nuclear technology to developing nations.

⑤ British Prime Minister Tony Blair said he would probably be **clinging to** the doorknocker when he actually quits office to face life as a "former celebrity," in an interview published yesterday. Blair said he felt "all right so far" about his decision to **step down** on June 27 after more than a decade in power, in an interview with novelist Martin Amis for The Guardian.

Unit 39 Passives

GRAMMAR NOTES

(1) The types of the passives

- The dog *was saved* by its owner. (verbal passive)
- Mary *was* (*very*) *surprised at* the news. (adjectival passive)
- This bed *has not been slept in / on / under / near.* (prepositional)
- The glass shattered. (middle voice)
- They *got killed* by the hijackers. (*get*-passive)
  cf. They *got* very *frightened.*
- Mary *had* her purse *snatched.* (passive (S: experiencer) / causative)
- He *is offended by* crude language. (long passive)
- The village *was destroyed.* (short passive)

(2) Degrees of transitivity

- Cameron *smashed* the truck. → The truck was smashed by Cameron.
- Manny *hated* the movie. → ?The movie was hated by Manny.
- The baby likes the cookies. → ??The cookies are liked by the baby.

(3) 'middle' voice

There is a 'middle voice' intermediate between active and passive voices. The middle voice allows the subject of a sentence to be nonagentive, as in the passive voice, but the morphology of the verb to be in the active voice.

- This book *reads* well.
- The shirt *irons* well.
- The meat *cut* surprisingly easily.
- She doesn't *frighten* easily.
  (*bend, cook, hammer, keep, open, turn, wash,* ⋯)

(4) Passive only

- Mehdi *was born* in Tehran.
- Your order *was shipped* on July 10th by first class mail.
  (*be deemed, be fined, be hospitalized, be jailed, be scheduled, be shipped, be suspended,* ⋯)
- *It is rumored* that he will get the job. (complex passive)
- It *is reported* that the finance minister is to resign.

GRAMMATICAL EXPLORATION IN CONTEXT

① The five whales — four adult females and one yearling male — have been recovering in the Florida Keys for nearly four months. They will **be tagged** with electronic tracking devices and **monitored** in the water. If any doesn't thrive, it will **be recaptured** and **brought** back to the Keys.
(**yearling** (n): a young cow, deer, or horse that is between one and two years old)

② CHOOSE MY SEAT. Seats may **be pre-assigned** on Northwest-operated flights a maximum of 90 days prior to departure. Premium seats **are blocked** on most aircraft for customers with WorldPerks/Alliance Partner Elite status or a business fare purchase. Select seats are also available for customers with special needs, unaccompanied minors or families traveling with small children. Seats can **be selected** at the time of making reservations.
(**premium** (adj): more expensive or of higher quality than other similar things)

③ The Thermotex heating pad is safe to use and its use has no known side effects. The Thermotex heating pad **is now being offered** to the public in all of Canada and in the United States. Thousands **are being sold** with rave reviews from consumers. Testimonials from a few of these consumers **are** also **published** on this page.

④ In rural Pennsylvania, church bells began tolling solemnly shortly after 10 a.m., marking the moment hijacked Flight 93 crashed in a field near Shanksville as passengers tried to fight off their hijackers. The plane **was believed to be headed** to the nation's capital.

⑤ Isabel has been **weakening** for days, but it remained a potent force capable of downing trees and producing heavy flooding once it reaches land. (hurricane Isabel)

Unit 40 *Get* - passives

GRAMMAR NOTES

(1) *Get*-passives

The *get*-passive is quite common in informal, conversational English.

- Kim *got mauled* by our neighbor's dog. (*get*-passive)
  cf. Kim *was mauled* by our neighbor's dog. (*be*-passive)
- They are *getting married* next month.
- Barry *got invited* to the party.
- Is it more difficult to *get admitted* to some colleges than others?
- I *got arrested* for drunken driving last week.
- My dog *got bitten* by a snake.
- They *got mugged* by some teenagers.
- The unruly students *got punished*.
- There was a fight at the party but nobody *got hurt*.
- My wife *got fired*.
- Our dog *got run over* by a car.
- Step back or you'll *get hit* by the ball.
- She *got* herself *caught*.
- "*Did* Bruno *get arrested*?" "No, he didn't even *get caught*."

(2) *Have* / *get* something *done*

- We *had* / *got* the car *delivered* to the airport. (= It was delivered)
  cf. We *had delivered* the car to the airport. (= We delivered the car)
- While I was Singapore I *had* / *got* my eyes *tested*. (= They were tested)
- "I'd like to make a small withdrawal from my bank account."
  "I*'ve got* your balance *pulled up* on my computer."
- That pipe has been leaking for ages. We must *get* it *mended*.

(3) *The* differences between *be*-passive and *get*-passive

The *be*-passive is prototypical passive verb and it is unmarked and semantically neutral, which is not true of the *get*-passive. The *get*-passive overwhelmingly tends to be used adversely and thus occurs with verbs from semantic categories such as physical assault (*get hit*), hindrance (*get rapped*), transference (*get snatched*), and verbs of emotional or mental strain (*get punished*), whose affinity for affective connotations is consistent with its colloquial nature.

GRAMMATICAL EXPLORATION IN CONTEXT 

① "We wanted to reflect the real atmosphere of life in Iraq. You could **get kidnapped** here any time. Or a bomb could kill you. This is our life."

② "If someone is coming at you with a knife, if you can't retreat, you do what you have to do. We do not put officers out there to **get hurt**," he said.

(**retreat** (v): to move away from something or someone **put out**: if you **put someone out**, you cause them trouble or inconvenience because they have to do something for you. **officer** (n): police officer)

③ Tape the opening of your box and reinforce all seams with 2" wide tape. Use clear or brown packaging tape, reinforced packing tape or paper tape. Do not use cord, string or twine because they **get caught** in mail processing equipment.

④ Now that actor-director Kevin Costner is back with *Open Range* in theaters, will we see more from him? And did I hear he's **getting married**?

⑤ Particularly, it was her strong leadership and outstanding credentials that **got her elected**, winning the respect and trust from other fellow scientists.

Unit 41 Participle clauses

GRAMMAR NOTES

(1) The semantic categories of participle clauses

- *Opening her eyes,* the baby began to cry. (time)
- *Cleared*, the site will be very valuable. (= When it is cleared, …)
- It's a trick I learned *while recovering* from an illness.
- The fruit was expensive, *being imported.* (reason)
- *Unhappy* with the decision, Johnson swore at the referee.
- *A man of few words*, Uncle George declined to express an opinion.
- *Looked after carefully*, the plant can live through the winter. (condition)
- *Cleared*, the site would be very valuable. (= If it were cleared, …)
- *Understanding* her problem, I don't know how I can help. (concessive)
- *Though defeated*, she remained a popular leader of the party.
  (= Though she had been defeated, …)
- Using a sharp axe, they broke down the door. (means) (= By using …)
- I used to lie awake at night, *worrying* about the next exam.
- *Answering* a poll on driver attitudes and behaviors, respondents admitted to regularly engaging in dangerous driving practices.
- *Not wishing* to go out that night, I made an excuse.
- *The weather having improved,* the game was enjoyed by players and spectators alike.
- *His remark having been represented* as an insult, Mr. Anderson was later forced to resign from the committee.
- *The job finished*, we went home straight away.
- Store in a cool, dry place *with lid tightly closed.*
- *With more students demanding and paying for privacy,* the roommate is no longer the staple of college life it once was.
- *Whether right or wrong*, he usually wins the argument.
  (= Whether he is right or wrong ….)

(2) Restrictive and nonrestrictive participle clauses

- The bus drivers *rejecting the management offer* remained on strike.
  (= The bus drivers *who rejected* …… remained on strike.)
- The bus drivers, *rejecting the management offer,* remained on strike.
  (= The bus drivers, *who rejected* ……, remained on strike.)

GRAMMATICAL EXPLORATION IN CONTEXT 

① Once **known** as white gold because it was such a profitable crop, cotton is no longer a money-making venture in India.

② Had I known about Dermalogica's new line of sun care products, maybe I wouldn't have been as hesitant to go on beach trips as I was this summer. And **knowing** that I now have more of a chance against premature aging, I can go back to looking at the mirror without trepidation.

③ My wife works late but always comes home cheerful, **shouting**, "Honey, I'm home!" Our two-year-old daughter has decided to adopt this as her favorite phrase. Last month she excitedly came through the door from her first day of preschool **mimicking** her mother, **saying,** "Honey, I'm home!"

④ **With Hurricane Isabel approaching** the mid-Atlantic region and **expected** to affect Pennsylvania by late Thursday, Penn State is advising students, faculty and staff at all campus locations to keep a watchful eye on the storm. (**keep an eye on**: take care of, watch carefully)

⑤ California Governor Arnold Schwarzenegger lit a cigar during his trip to Canada this week, but did he break US law? The celebrity governor known for his love for premium cigars was in Ottawa last week on his way to the airport when his motorcade made a detour to a hotel. There, Schwarzenegger picked up a Cuban cigar in a shop, **with the bill paid** by an aide traveling with him, the *Ottawa Citizen* reported. US citizens are prohibited from buying Cuban cigars anywhere in the world.

Unit 42 Infinitives

GRAMMAR NOTES

(1) Distinction between infinitives and gerunds

In general, infinitives represent *intentions, desires*, or *expectations*, (*neutrality*) and gerunds represent *facts*. The association of *fact* with gerunds and of *intention* with infinitives can help you know in the majority of cases whether to use an infinitive or a gerund when another verb immediately precedes it. The distinction between fact and intention (*neutrality*) is not a rule but only a tendency, and it can be superseded by other rules.

- It's best for Sarah *to be patient*. (It's best *if* Sarah is patient.)
- He likes me *to work* late. (and that's why I do it.' or 'but I never do it.)
- He likes me *working* late. (and that's why I do it.)
- I'm surprised at *his making that mistake*. (··· surprised *that* he made ···.)

(2) Grammatical patterns

(a) verb + *to*-infinitive
- We've decided *to leave* early. (*agree, consent, expect, fail, hope, manage, offer, pretend, refuse, start, threaten, volunteer, want,* ···)

(b) verb + object + *to*-infinitive
- The police warned *everyone to stay* inside with their windows closed. (*advise, allow, believe, cause, command, enable, encourage, entitle, force, invite, order, order, persuade, remind, show, teach, tell,* ···)

(c) verb + *for* object + *to*-infinitive
- They *arranged for* Jane *to stay* in London. (*apply, arrange, ask, campaign, long, plan, wait,* ···)

(d) verb + object + bare infinitive
- She noticed him run away from the house. (*feel, have, hear, notice, observe, overhear, see, watch / have, make, let, ...*)

(3) *to*-infinitive: passive forms

- The law needs *to be revised* if justice is *to be done.*
- Kevin hoped *to be selected* by the team captain. (*appear, begin, come, continue, seem, tend / agree, aim, attempt, hope, refuse, struggle, try,* ···)

GRAMMATICAL EXPLORATION IN CONTEXT

① When it comes to spoiling our furry friends, there's no shortage of affection. We cuddle them, we take them with us when we travel – some of us even throw birthday parties for our dogs and cats. But perhaps the best way **to love** your animals is **to use** preventative measures **to ensure** a healthy aging process. (**cuddle**: hug)

② "I have found the president to be **an easy** man **to talk to**. He expresses his opinions clearly and he's **easy to understand**," Bush said. "One thing is for certain, we will work to have the best possible relations between our two countries."

③ "Our tracking hikes are open to all ages, and we try to make each one an adventure. Our goal is **for people to feel** more attuned to the natural world around them," says Crilley. (**attuned** (adj): (never before noun) familiar with something and able to deal with it in a sensitive way)

④ Bill Clinton is nothing if not persistent. He gets goals, and I was one of them. He asked me **to marry him again**, and again, and I always said no. Eventually he said, "Well, I'm not going to ask you **to marry me any more**, and if you ever decide you want **to marry me** then you have to tell me." He would wait me out. (**wait out**: to stay where you are until something ends, usually something bad: *Let's go to the basement and wait out the storm there.*)

⑤ Human beings need **to be loved** and **cared for**. When warm feelings exist between people, it is natural **to give** and **receive love**. In fact, a common proverb is: "It is better **to give** than **to receive**."
Children who do well in school seem **to be receiving** strong and consistent love and support from their families. On the other hand, many antisocial adolescents appear **not to have received** much tender, loving care during their childhood.

Unit 43 Gerunds

GRAMMAR NOTES

(1) Positions of gerunds

- *Her drinking* disturbs me.
- *The first warning* has been issued.
- Tucker loves *swimming in the ocean.*
- I can't stand *their incessant criticizing.*
- He was ticketed for *dangerous driving.*
- In today's hectic world, one of the biggest challenges is *maintaining* a balanced lifestyle, with proper diet and regular exercise.
- They are busy *preparing* a barbecue.

(2) Grammatical patterns

(a) verb + ~ *ing*

- We sincerely appreciated *having* you with us and wish you good luck.
- I am considering *solving* all our troubles by going back home.

(*admit, avoid, appreciate, consider, delay, deny, detest, dislike, , dread, enjoy, feel like, finish, imagine, loathe, miss, propose, put off, recall, resent, risk, suggest,* ···)

(b) verb + (object) + ~*ing*

- She remembers *seeing* him leave an hour ago.
- I won't stand them *interrupting* me all the time.

(*can't / won't stand, detest, hate, imagine, keep, like, love, mind, regret, remember,* ···)

(3) Implied subject of ~*ing* clause

- I objected to *his / Jeremy's* receiving an invitation. (formal)
- I objected to *him / Jeremy* receiving an invitation. (informal)
- Do you remember *my/me* loaning you that book?
- *My* forgetting her name is embarrassing.
- I dislike *Eric('s)* wearing my clothes.
- I don't like *people telling* me how to do things better.
- I don't know about *the weather* being so awful in this area.

(4) Gerund: passive forms

- I really love being giv*en* presents.
- The children enjoyed being taken to the zoo.

GRAMMATICAL EXPLORATION IN CONTEXT

① Up until now your first child has had your undivided attention and love. So **having a sibling** will seem like a real loss for her. At the same time, it will also be a big gain. Siblings help children learn about **sharing** and cooperation, and they can be a source of friendship and support for the rest of their lives. (**undivided** (adj): (only before noun) complete)

② Do you choose fashion over comfort? I'll choose comfort. You can buy outfits that are fashionable, yet comfortable. It feels great to look good but we should also consider **being** comfortable with what we are wearing.

③ Every year, New Jersey's wildlife contributes to our economy by **attracting** millions of people who enjoy all kinds of recreational opportunities from **hunting** and **fishing** to **hiking** and **bird watching**. (**wildlife** (n): animals, birds, and plants that live in natural conditions)

④ Women complain (rightly) of centuries of exploitation. Yet, to an economist, women are not exploited enough: they are the world's most underutilized resource; **getting** more of them into work is part of the solution to many economic woes. In developing countries where girls are less likely to go to school than boys, **investing** in education would deliver huge economic and social returns.

⑤ I have been using Sekkisei for three years now and I must say that my skin has never looked brighter. It is not about **transforming** your skin into a white J-pop princess. It is more of **removing** dullness, **preventing** freckles caused by sunburn and **maintaining** a healthy skin condition in a gentle manner. (**J-pop princess**: Japanese pop music princess)

Unit 44 Simple present

GRAMMAR NOTES

It is a peculiarity of English that a present simple tense form cannot normally be used to refer to an ongoing action in present time:

(1) Present state

- I*'m* awfully busy. / *Do* you *like* my hat?

(2) Present habit, timeless present

- He *works* all the time – he never relaxes.
- Stress *causes* high blood pressure. / The earth *moves* round the sun.

(3) Fixed, unchangeable events

- The next semester *begins* in three weeks.
- 'What time *does* the movie begin?' 'It *begins* at 8:30.'

(4) The future: temporal or conditional clause

- I should be finished *by the time* you *get* back.
- He'll do it if you *pay* him.

(5) The historic present

- This lady yesterday, she *says* 'I can't believe this …'
- Then in *comes* the bartender and *tries* to stop the fight.

(6) Verbs of communication (*explain, hear, inform, say, see, tell, understand,* …)

- I *hear* you've finished the building project.
- The doctor *says* he thinks I had a mild concussion.

(7) Currently ongoing actions

The present simple tense form is used to denote a currently ongoing action, involving formal declarations (performative verbs), demonstrations, sports commentaries, and present-tense narratives.

- I *declare* the meeting closed.
- You *hold* the can in one hand. Right, you're holding it on one hand; now you *take off* the lid with the other.
- King *serves* to the left-hand court and Adams *makes* a wonderful return. She's playing magnificent tennis in this match ….
- I was sitting in the park, reading a newspaper, when all of a sudden this dog *jumps* at me.

GRAMMATICAL EXPLORATION IN CONTEXT

① Describe your personal style: My style **varies** on my mood but I also **dress** in another way when **I'm** out. I **dress** more fashionable when I'm out shopping, having dinner, and meeting up with friends. However, I **prefer** wearing plain tees, jeans, and flip flops when going to school.

② Psychologists **describe** two major personality types - Type A and Type B. People with Type A personalities **work** very hard. They never **relax**. They usually **rush** through their daily activities. They **get** angry easily and often **have** high blood pressure. In contrast, Type B personalities usually **take** life easier. They **remain** calm even in stressful situations and rarely **lose** their tempers.

③ Beginning Monday, users will be able to keep their phone numbers when they **change** cell companies. Also, if they **want** to get rid of their landline phones, they can transfer the numbers to cell phones.
(**landline phones**: a telephone that is not a mobile phone)

④ Hiking Mount Nittany By the Season. ······ IN FALL, birches, ashes, hickories, and some maples **turn** yellow. Oaks **follow** from bronze to dark red. IN WINTER, leafless trees along ridge trails **offer** additional valley views. Snow **shows** deer, fox, turkey and bear tracks. Woodpeckers **abound**.

⑤ North Korea and the United States **have** no diplomatic relations and **are** technically in the middle of a state of war interrupted by a 51-year armistice. The United States **insists** that North Korea **dismantle** its nuclear program. The North **says** it first **wants** economic and humanitarian aid and assurances that Washington won't attack.

Unit 45 Simple past

GRAMMAR NOTES

(1) The event at a definite time in the past

The past tense is used when the past happening is related to a definite time, in the past ('past-happening-related-to-past time'), which may be identified by (i) a past-time adverbial in the same sentence, (ii) the preceding language context, or (iii) the context outside language:

- The Israeli Prime Minister *flew* into New York yesterday to start his visit to the US.
- He *died* more than ten years ago.
- John has become engaged; it *took* us completely by surprise.
- Jim Cooper has died of cancer; he *was* 68 and *lived* in Texas ⋯.
- *Did* you *get* any letters?
- Hello, how are you? They *told* me you were ill.

(2) Habitual and regular actions, completed events in the past

- We *walked* a great deal in my boyhood.
- *Did* you drive *past* her house every day?
- We *went* to Spain three times last year.
- She *got up* when the alarm clock *went off.*
- He *jumped* out of bed and *ran* to see who the parcel was for.

(3) Substitution for simple present or present perfect form

(a) The simple past and past progressive are indirect and more tactful substitute for the simple present form.

- *Did* you want to speak to me? (= Do you want ⋯?)
- I *wondered* whether you would help me. (= I wonder ⋯)
- I *was wondering* if you would like to go out to dinner tonight.
  (= I *wonder* / I *am wondering* / I *wondered* ⋯.)

(b) There is an idiomatic use of the past tense with *always, ever* and *never* to refer to a state or habit leading up to the present:

- I *always said* (= have said) he would end up in jail.
- *Did* you *ever taste* that seaweed?

GRAMMATICAL EXPLORATION IN CONTEXT

① The pop star's arrival outside the courthouse, at about 8:40 a.m. Pacific time, **was** 10 minutes later than scheduled. Members of Mr. Jackson's family, including his father, as well as his defense team, had already shown up when the sports utility vehicle bearing the singer **arrived**.

② Edward Teller, who **was** present at the creation of the first nuclear weapons and who **grew** even more famous for defending them, **died** yesterday at his home on the Stanford University campus in Palo Alto, Calif., according to the Lawrence Livermore National Laboratory, which Dr. Teller once **headed**. He **was** 95.

③ Nearly 140 years ago, two great armies **met** on the rolling hills of south central Pennsylvania and when three days had passed this small town **marched** into history as the site of the greatest battle ever fought in the Americas. Our nation **was** forged anew at Gettysburg.

④ Kevin Millwood **pitched** eight impressive innings and the Philadelphia Phillies **ended** their season-high six-game losing streak, defeating the New York Mets 7-0 tonight.

⑤ I never **thought** **I'd** come to dread looking at the mirror. Just recently, I **discovered** a spider web of very fine lines on one side of my face. I **panicked**. I just **celebrated** my birthday a month ago and this discovery **downplayed** the celebratory aspect, as if the lines **were** taunting reminders that I **was** slowly slinking into the late twenties category and **was** not exempted from anything being in this age group signifies.

Unit 46 Present progressive

GRAMMAR NOTES

(1) Ongoing, incomplete, and temporary event in the present time

(a) the moment of speaking

- At the moment, Taro *is speaking* English.
- "Who *are* you *phoning*?" "*I'm trying* to get through to Helen."
- We*'re having* a meeting. Come and join us.

(b) emphasizing the present moment

- We*'re trying* to create a more democratic society.
- I'*m working* as a British Council Officer.
- She*'s spending* the summer in Europe.

(c) progressive change

- The village *is changing* but it is still undisturbed.
- *Is* your English *getting* better?

(d) habitual actions

- 'You'*re drinking* too much.' – 'Only at home. No one sees me but you.'
- Do you know if she*'s* still *playing* these days?
- She*'s writing* some short stories. (temporariness)
  cf. She writes short stories. (permanence)

(e) the future

- The train is leaving at nine (tomorrow).
- We're having a party next Saturday.

(2) The present progressive with some state verbs

(a) some state verbs (*attract, like, live, look, love, sound,* …) and psych-verbs (mental state verbs) (*find, realize, regret, think, understand,* …): temporary or dynamic meanings

- Jean's with us at the moment. The children *are loving* having her here.
- I *am living* with some friends until I can find an apartment.
- I'*m regretting* my decision to give her the job.
- I'*m understanding* statistics better these days.
- I *am thinking* about dessert.

(b) verbs with emotion or attitude: tentativeness

- I'*m hoping* to take my exam soon.
- I *was wondering* whether you could help me.

GRAMMATICAL EXPLORATION IN CONTEXT

① Major airlines, which have lost billions of dollars since the Sept. 11 terrorist attacks in New York and Washington, **are looking** for ways to better compete with the low-fare airlines.

② The long-awaited Thanksgiving break is finally here, and most Penn State students are ready to go home. This year, only 30 students **are staying** in dorms for break, while last year 70 students took advantage of this option. Members of several Penn State sports teams **are also staying** for part of the break.

③ Federal, state and local officials **are working** to recover the thousands of pieces of debris spread across Texas and Louisiana, and NASA engineers **are poring** over mounds of data, trying to understand what happened in the moments before Columbia disintegrated in the skies above Texas on Saturday morning.

④ The top U.S. military commander for the Persian Gulf region said yesterday that terrorism **is becoming** the "number one security threat" in Iraq, with foreign fighters entering the country through Syria and a revived group called Ansaral-Islam now firmly established in Baghdad.

⑤ I'**m working** very hard these days, but I have some good news. Right now, **I'm sitting** at a desk in the Entertainment Section of the Tribune! Of course **I'm** still **taking** journalism classes at night as well. The job is temporary - Joe Sims, the regular reporter, **is taking** this month off to write a book. This week we**'re preparing** to interview your favorite group, the Airheads. In fact, at this very moment they**'re flying** into town by helicopter. They'**re performing** at the King Theater all week. How **are** you **doing**? **Are** you still **writing** music? Oops! The crew **is calling** me. They'**re leaving** for the theater now. Write soon!

Unit 47 Past progressive

GRAMMAR NOTES

(1) Temporary past actions

- I *was working* in a car factory during the summer of 2005.
  cf. He worked hard all his life.
- Sally *was reading* to the children while Kevin *was washing up.*

(2) Repeated past actions

- Her tooth *was aching*, her burnt finger *was hurting.*
- He *was looking* ill.
- When Carlo was in hospital, we *were visiting* him twice a week.
- Everyone *was begging* the captain to surrender.

(3) Contrasting events

- We *were* all *sitting* round the fire waiting for my soldier to come home. He *arrived* about six in the evening.
- I *was waiting* angrily on Monday morning when I *saw* Mrs. Miller.

(4) Unachieved intention in the past

- We *were meaning to* call in and see you, but Jane wasn't feeling well. (or we *meant to* …)
- I *had hoped* to visit the gallery before I left Florence, but it's closed on Sundays. (or *I hoped* …, *I was hoping* …, *I had been hoping* …)
  (*expect to, hope to, intend to, plan to, want to, consider ~ing, plan on ~ing, think about/of ~ ing*)

(4) The future; the past or present progressive

- I *was thinking of* going down to London next weekend, but it depends how much money I've got. (less definite)
  cf. I'*m thinking* of going down to … (more definite)
- We *were wondering* about inviting Kay over tomorrow.
  cf. We'*re wondering* about …
  (*hope to, intend to, plan to, want to, consider ~ing, plan on ~ing, think about/of ~ ing* and *wonder about*)

GRAMMATICAL EXPLORATION IN CONTEXT

① CIA officials said at the time that they had reliable information that Saddam, his two sons and other top Iraqi leaders **were meeting** there.

② The president **was leaving** Monday for New Jersey where he planned to speak to the business community before returning to the White House.

③ (The police are questioning a burglary suspect)
Police: What **were** you **doing** last Tuesday between 6:00 and 9:00 p.m.?
Suspect: Well, let's see. I **was** probably **doing** what I always do. I was with my wife. We **were eating** dinner. We finished around 7:00.
P: OK. So what **were** you **doing** between 7:00 and 9:00?
S: Between 7:00 and 9:00? I **was watching** TV.
P: And what **was** your wife **doing** while you **were watching** TV?

④ "We encourage the kids who are involved in our animal tracking activities to imagine what the animal **was feeling** when it left those tracks – **was it being pursued**, **was it pursuing** another animal, how **it was relating** to its natural environment," says Kirsten Werner of Tyler Arboretum in Media, Pennsylvania.

⑤ I **was buying** a new alarm clock the other day in Taylor's the jewelers, when I actually saw somebody shoplifting. I'd just finished paying for my clock and as I turned round, an elderly woman **was** slowly **putting** a silver plate into a bag that she **was carrying**. Then she walked over to another part of the shop and picked up an expensive-looking watch a number of times. When she thought that nobody **was looking**, she dropped it into the bag. Before I had a chance to tell the staff in the shop, she noticed that I **was watching** her and hurried out. Unfortunately for her, two police officers **were walking** past just at that moment and she ran straight into them.

Unit 48 Present perfect

GRAMMAR NOTES

The perfect aspect is used for a past happening which is seen in relation to a later event or time. Thus the present perfect means 'past-happening-related-to-the-present-time':

- They *have been* married for ten years. (this probably means 'They are still married.')

(1) Past event with results in the present time: the most common use.

- The taxi *has arrived.* (i.e. 'it's now here')
- All police leave *has been cancelled.* (i.e. 'the police remain on duty')
- Her doll *has been broken.* (i.e. 'it's still not mended')

cf. Her doll *was broken*, but now it's mended.

(2) Indefinite events in a period leading up to the present time

- *Have* you (ever) *been* to Florida?
- All the family *have suffered* from the same illness (in the last five years)

(3) Habit in a period leading up to the present time

- She *has attended* lectures regularly this term.
- He*'s played* regularly at Wimbledon since he was eighteen.

(4) State leading up to the present time

- She *has owned* the house since her father died.
- They *have been* unhappy for a long time.

(5) Adverbials in relation to the present perfect

- I *haven't had* any luck *since* I was baby.
- Plenty of rain *has fallen* here *lately.*
- So far he *has done* nothing to speak of.
- *Up to now* her life *hasn't been* altogether rosy.

(6) Present time expressions; *this morning, etc.*

Time expressions that refer to the present, such as *this morning / week / month* and *today*, can be used with either simple past or present perfect.

- I *had* two cups of coffee this morning. (= the morning is over)
- I'*ve had* two cups of coffee this morning. (= it is still the morning)

GRAMMATICAL EXPLORATION IN CONTEXT 

① Security **has been raised** to a higher alert at University Park Airport since the start of the war with Iraq, but there **hasn't been** much change in the number of people traveling.

② Abby, I **have learned** many things from this experience. I **have learned** that smiles on my children's faces are far more important than shiny floors and sparkling windows. I **have** also **learned** that giving help is as important as receiving it.

③ Machine-made snow **has been** substantially **refined** by the ski industry over the years. Snowmaking serves to extend the ski season or can rescue a dry winter, but it also **has become** important for controlling snow conditions as the number of skiers **has increased** and the mode of enjoying the slopes **has evolved** to include tubing, sledding, and snowboarding. Machine snow is also used in labs to learn how to forecast avalanches.

④ SAN FRANCISCO — Former major leaguer Bobby Bonds, father of slugger Barry Bonds, **has died**, the San Francisco Giants said. The senior Bonds — one of baseball's best all-around players during the 1970s — **was** 57 and **had been** ill for nearly a year with a brain tumor and lung cancer. (**all-around** (adj): *AmE* good at doing a lot of different things, especially in sports.)

⑤ Collins said her crew had thoroughly studied the procedures before Wednesday's unprecedented spacewalk when astronaut Stephen Robinson removed two worrisome pieces of filler material from the shuttle's belly**. It was the first time** an astronaut **has ventured** below the ship. (**worrisome** (adj): worried, worrying)

Unit 49 Present perfect progressive

GRAMMAR NOTES

(1) Emphasizing duration of event

(a) The present perfect progressive expresses the idea of *activity in progress* until recently or until the time of speaking.

- I'*ve been reading* your book (normally = 'I'm still reading it').
  cf. I'*ve read* your book (= 'I've finished it').
- *Have* you *been working* in the garden all day? You look exhausted.
- What *have* you *been doing*, sleeping all day?
- She'*s been explaining* to me what you're doing.

(b) We don't use the present perfect progressive with **stative verbs** (*belong, know, (dis)like, understand,* ···)

- I *haven't liked* ice cream since I ate too much and was sick.
- *Have* you *known* each other long?
- We*'ve had* it for fifteen years.

(2) The present perfect progressive vs. present perfect

(a) The present perfect progressive emphasizes that an activity is **ongoing and repeated**, while the present perfect suggests that the activity happened only once or on a specified number of occasions:

- Joseph *has been kicking* a football against the wall all day.
- He *has played* for the national team in 65 matches so far.

(b) The perfect progressive, like the simple perfect, can suggest that the results of the activity remain in the present: *You've been fighting*! In such cases the activity has continued up to the recent past, not up to the present.

- You look like you*'ve been crying*.
- Your eyes are red – *have* you *been crying*?
- 'You looked tired.' 'I*'ve been washing* clothes all day.'
- I *have been swimming* and I feel exhausted.
- You*'ve been eating* chocolate, haven't you? There's some on your shirt.
- Who*'s been messing* around with my papers? They're all over the place.

GRAMMATICAL EXPLORATION IN CONTEXT

① Tensions **have been growing** since October, when Pyongyang acknowledged privately to Kelly that it had restarted its nuclear weapons program.

② For months, Washington **has been trying** to convince Asian nations, especially South Korea and China, that the North Korean threat is so urgent that it requires a unified diplomatic front to force the country to give up its weapons.

③ For weeks, negotiators **have been discussing** a U.S. offer for aid that would help the Turkish economy if there were a war in neighboring Iraq. Turkey fears that a conflict could devastate its tourism industry, which brings in some $10 billion a year.

④ For years, Divot's regional golf magazines **have been supporting** the game of golf and the great courses in New England that enable us all to enjoy the sport we love – rain or shine.

⑤ (*Dr. Petra Adams, the Director of the Center, talks to a reporter*)
It's remarkable to think that since 1950 influenza has claimed more than 50,000 lives in this country, and in 1957 alone around 6,000 people died. But over the last 20 years we at the Center **have been making** considerable progress on understanding the illness. We've produced over a hundred books and articles reporting the results of our research and in 1995 they awarded the Nobel Prize for medicine to one of my colleagues. In our more recent work we**'ve been looking** into the effects of influenza on heart disease and we**'ve** also **been exploring** a possible link between climate change and the recent increase in the number of cases of influenza. It is a tragedy that the government has made this decision now.

Unit 50 Past perfect

GRAMMAR NOTES

(1) 'Past in the past'

- They (*had*) *moved* into the house before the baby was born.
- The house *had been* empty for several months (when we bought it).
- His parents *had been married* for twelve years when he was born.
- When he stopped laughing, everyone *had left.* (= they left before he stopped laughing)

  cf. When he stopped laughing, everyone *left.* (= they left after he stopped laughing)
- I *had known* Megan since we were at school together.
- She *had owned* the house since her parents died. (she does not own it now)

  cf. She *has owned* the house since her parents died. (she still owns it)

(2) Finished activity before a past time:

- I'*d finished* all the ironing so I started cleaning the windows.
- He *had already* left before I could offer him a ride.

(3) *How many* times:

- How many times *had* you *met* him before yesterday?
- I *had stayed* in the hotel twice in the 1990s.

(4) Time expressions: if the order of past events is clear from the context we can often use either past perfect or simple past:

- After Ivan (*had*) *finished* reading, he *put out* the light.
- They were given help and advice before they (*had*) *made* the decision.
- She *had* just *stepped* into her office when the telephone *rang.*
- She *became* famous after she *appeared* on the TV program.

(5) Special uses

(a) indirect reporting

- I told her the parcel *had not* arrived.
- The Secretary of State said that he *had spoken* to both sides, urging restraint.

(b) attitudinal past perfect

- I *had wondered* whether you *are* / *were* free now.

  cf. I *wondered* / *wonder* whether you are free now.

GRAMMATICAL EXPLORATION IN CONTEXT

① Mr. Blair replied he was not there to answer questions on Vietnam, which **had not been** subject to UN resolutions.
(**subject to**: in a situation where you have to obey a rule or law)

② Yellowstone officials said the park's east entrance, which **had been** closed for about a week and a half because of fire, would reopen on a limited basis Sunday.

③ BEIJING, April 25 - China sought today to put a positive face on the talks it arranged between the United States and North Korea, but diplomats and analysts argued that North Korea **had alienated** China, its only significant ally, by declaring that it **had already become** a nuclear power.
(**put a brave / good / positive face on**: If you put a brave / good / positive face on a bad situation, or put on a brave / good / positive face, you try not to show how disappointed or upset you are about the situation. **alienate** (v): to make someone dislike you, or not want to help or support you)

④ As it was making landfall in North Carolina, Isabel already **had caused** the cancellation of hundreds of airline flights in and out of airports in North Carolina, Virginia and the three major airports around Washington.
(**landfall** (n): the time when a storm or hurricane arrives on time)

⑤ Still, Powell told the council the time for action **had arrived**, and repeated the administration's assertions that Hussein is strengthening terrorist ties.

Unit 51 Past perfect progressive

GRAMMAR NOTES

(1) an ongoing action over a period of time in the past prior to some other past event or time:

- Carol *had been working* hard, so her doctor told her to take a vacation.
- She *had been wearing* high-heeled shoes, and her feet hurt.
- Tom gave up smoking five years ago. He*'d been smoking* for 30 years.
- He *had been applying* for the job, without success, since leaving university.
- Since then, the mother *had been living* with her daughter.
- The rain *had been pouring* all night.

(2) a situation or activity that went on before a particular past time and (a) finished at that time, (b) continued beyond it, or (c) finished shortly before it:

- We*'d been driving* for an hour when the engine suddenly stopped.
- She felt terrible during the interview because she *had been suffering* from flu since the previous day.
- When I last saw John, he*'d been running* and was out of breath.

(3) We don't describe *states* with progressive tenses, even when we focus on the length of a situation up to a particular past time:

- We *had owned* the car for 6 months before we discovered it was stolen.
- I *had* always *believed* it would be easy to get a job, and was disappointed to be rejected.

(4) unachieved intention in the past

- Bill *had been planning* to retire at 60, but we have persuaded him to stay for a few more years. (Bill *had planned* ···, Bill *was planning* ···, Bill *planned*, ···)
- I *had hoped* to leave by 9.00, but I overslept and missed the train.

GRAMMATICAL EXPLORATION IN CONTEXT 

① Pyongyang **had been insisting** on one-on-one negotiations with the United States but ultimately accepted a U.S. proposal for a broad international negotiation.

② Turkey **had been asking** for $10 billion in grants and $20 billion in loans. The United States **had been offering** $6 billion in grants. A Western diplomat said each billion in grants could guarantee $10 billion in loans.

③ When August Blanchard returned to New Orleans from Pennsylvania in late December, his mother was still missing. Family members, scattered across the country, **had been calling** hospitals, the Red Cross and missing persons hot lines, hoping she **had been rescued**.

④ The car the woman **had been driving** was found parked on the Ocean City-Longport Bridge early on the morning of Jan. 15. There was no sign of either Codario-Ferrino or her daughter when investigators arrived at the scene. The keys were still in the ignition of the 2002 Volkswagen Jetta, and Codario-Ferrino's pocketbook was found on the passenger seat. (**scene** (v): (*usually singular*) a place where something happens, usually something bad. **at / on the scene**)

⑤ A senior Ugandan official said Monday that Sudanese Vice President John Garang has been confirmed dead in a helicopter crash in southern Sudan. Ugandan and Sudanese forces **had been searching** for Garang's helicopter since Sunday. Uganda's president said it had crashed in bad weather in the border region between the two countries.

Unit 52 Future expressions

GRAMMAR NOTES

Future time is expressed by means of *modal auxiliaries, modal idioms,* and *semi-auxiliaries,* or by *the simple present* and *progressive forms*. The most important future constructions are those which use *will* and *be going to*. Of these, *will* is by far the most common option, particularly in writing.

(1) Will

- He *will* be here in half an hour. (prediction)
- I *think* he *will* arrive tomorrow. (*bet, expect, hope, imagine, wonder,* …)
- The meeting *will* begin at 9.00 a.m. Refreshments *will* be available from 8.30 onwards. (formal)
- I am hoping that by the end of the month you *will have finished* your report.

(2) Simple present tense

- *Do* you *have* classes next Friday? (programmed arrangement)
- The term *finishes* at the beginning of July.
- I'll get her to phone you *when / if / after* she *comes* in.
- I hope the train *is* on time. / will be on time.
- Miss Walpole *retires* at the end of the year.

(3) Progressive aspect

- We*'re inviting* several people to a party. (definite arrangement)
- *Are* you *seeing* the doctor again next week? (firm intention)
- Don't call her at seven o'clock – They*'ll be eating* dinner then.
- Ann *will be helping* us to organize the party. (previous arrangement)
- Next year I *will have been working* in the company for 30 years.
- I*'ll be seeing* Tony on Tuesday. That's when we usually meet.
- When *will* you *be paying* back the money? (tentative)

(4) *Be to, be about to,* and *be on the point of ~ing*

- You *are not to leave* the school without my permission.
- North Korea today announced it *is to reactivate* a nuclear program frozen under a 1994 deal with the United States. (news reports)
- Another 385 people *are about to* lose their jobs.
- We were *on the point of leaving* when the phone rang.

GRAMMATICAL EXPLORATION IN CONTEXT

① Lorenz has plans to travel to California during the long weekend but she said the thought of work would follow her on vacation. "I **have** an exam a few days after we **come back**," she said. "I'**ll do** some on the plane, but I really **won't have** time to do work."

② When you **arrive** at Penn State, you **are to come** to our office for your welcome and check-in session. You should bring your passport, pink copy of your IAP-66 form, and I-94 card with you.

③ I teach on Tuesdays and Thursdays-so those days are pretty busy. Also, **I'll be leaving** for LA on Thursday evening to spend the weekend with my sister. It's her birthday and she really wants me to spend it with her. She**'s having** a big party on 9/28, the day of her birthday.

④ The women's soccer team **will be playing** UCLA Friday in Los Angeles. Calif., and **spending** the rest of their Thanksgiving break at the 2003 NCAA women's soccer tournament. The women's volleyball team **will be playing** at University of Minnesota on Friday and at the University of Iowa on Saturday.

⑤ We **get married** on the 26th, and I told the boys we**'re going to** have to train for the in-port race on the afternoon of the 27th. So we'**ll have** the morning, and that **will be** it. Presumably, with that 19.5-point lead and that wide hull, there **will be** longer celebrations ahead of the wedding party.

Unit 53 *Be going to*

GRAMMAR NOTES

(1) Present intention, previous decision

- Did you know that Bob and Kath *are going to* get married?
- Tony told me that she*'s going to* move back to Spain.
- I'*m not gonna* change my mind.
- I*'m going to* collect the children at 8.00.
- *Are* you *going to* talk at the meeting tonight?
- When *are* you *going to* get married?

(2) Prediction based on some present evidence or causative factors

- It's not a deep cut, but it*'s going to* leave a scar.
- 'What's the matter with her?' 'It looks like she*'s going to* faint.'
- *Are* you *going to* be all right, Mom?
- He *is going to* be doing a good job.
- I think I *am going to* have a cold.
- I'm afraid we*'re going to* have to stop the meeting now.
- You *are gonna* love it.
- Tomorrow *is going to* be a busy day for us.

(3) Permanent, uncontrollable situations

- Her new house *is going to / will* have three floors.
- People *are going to / will* live longer in the future. (* ··· are living ···)
- I think it*'s going to / will* rain soon. (*··· is raining ···)

(4) *Go / come + ~ ing*

- *Are* you *coming* home for lunch ? (* Are you going to come ···?)
- I*'m going to* town on Saturday. (* I'm going to go to town···)

(5) *Will / be going to*: little difference in meaning in (negative) if-clause

- We *will / are going to* study climate change in the next chapter.
- Where *will* you stay / *are* you *going to* stay in Portland?
- If we go on like this, we*'ll* / we*'re going to* lose all our money.
- You*'ll* / you*'re going to* knock that glass over if you're not more careful.

(6) *Will*: offers, requests, promises, etc. and ability in main clause (not *be going to*)

- If Jack phones I*'ll* let you know. (= offer)
- If you look to your left, you*'ll* see the lake. (= you'll be able to see)

GRAMMATICAL EXPLORATION IN CONTEXT

① He said all of the last minute work he encountered was stressful, but his break **is going to** be even more eventful. "I'**m going to** see my family, go to a wedding and then go hunting," Ogden said. "I have no time for rest and relaxation, but I don't mind because at least it's not work."

② "Does it make any sense to have a Democrat finish first and Republicans to finish second, third and fourth?" asked state Senate Minority Leader Jim Brulte on Friday. "At some point some of the leaders of the party **are going to** have to go to the candidates who **are going to** be nothing but a spoiler." (**spoiler** (n): (AmE) someone who spoils someone else's performance or success in an election or competition)

③ "I thought I **was going to** play well. I've been thinking about this tournament quite a lot," said Savarese. "I had a feeling something good **was going to** happen to me."

④ High winds that blew across the Great Lakes and into the Northeast delayed hundreds of flights at six of the nation's busiest airports Thursday and knocked out power to almost 1 million homes in eight states. "It's blowing pretty hard in a lot of places," said Paul Kocin, a winter weather expert for The Weather Channel. "**It's going to** impact tens of millions of people before it's through." (**knock out**: to destroy something or stop it working)

⑤ General Hoar recalled in an interview this week that he told Dr. Dean "that he was absolutely right, that the war was the wrong war at the wrong time, that it **was not going to** be easy, that we **were going to continue** to lose people, that it **was going to be** enormously expensive and that somebody in this administration needed to be held accountable for that." (**hold sb accountable / responsible / liable for**: to be responsible for)

Unit 54 Conjunctions

GRAMMAR NOTES

(1) Temporal clauses
- *As / When / While* Dave was eating, the doorbell rang.
- They were playing in the garden *when* they heard a scream.
- I still feel tired *when* I wake up in the morning. (every time)
- I had to wait six weeks *until / before* the parcel arrived.
- I had *no sooner* lighted the barbecue *than / when* it started to rain.
- Buy your ticket *as soon as* you reach the station.

(2) Reason clauses
- *As* Jane was the eldest, she had to look after her brothers and sisters.
- We have lunch early on Saturday *because* the girls are always in a hurry to go out.
- We hope to see much more of you *now that* you're living in Pusan.
- Ken just had to apologize, *seeing that / as / since* he knew he'd made a mistake.

(3) Purpose, result clauses
- I ignored his objections, *so* (*that*) he flew into a rage.
- They advertised the concert *so that* everyone should know about it.
- He left early *in case* he *should* miss the last train. (= ··· so that he should not miss it)

  cf. Take these pills, *in case* you feel ill on the boat.

(4) Concessive clauses
- We are enjoying ourselves, *though* the weather is bad.
- *While* we welcome his support, we disagree with a lot of his views.
- Elizabeth was lively and talkative, *whereas / while* her sister was quiet and reserved.
- Poor *that / as* they were, they gave money to charity.

(5) Similarity and comparison clauses
- Please do (exactly) *as* I said.
- It was just *like* I imagined it would be. (informal AmE)
- She looks *as if* she's getting better.
- She treated me *as though* I was / were / had been a stranger.
- Fill in the application form *as* instructed.

GRAMMATICAL EXPLORATION IN CONTEXT

① The People's bank of China warned again Thursday that it will take further steps to cool the economy as fixed-asset investments **for** the first five months of the year rose faster than expected.

② This fall **as** the leaves began to turn into an array of beautiful colors our family set off once again to pick apples from Willowpond Orchard in Sabattus. We have been going there **since before** we adopted our first daughter eight years ago from China. (**array** (n): *literary* beautiful or impressive clothes. **set off**: leave on a trip)

③ Cities are starting to treat trees less as decoration **and** more like public utilities **now that** they can calculate how much money trees save by cutting air pollution, storm runoff and energy costs.
(**public utilities**: a public service such as gas, water, or electricity. **runoff** (n): a flow of water or chemicals from one place to another, especially when this damages the environment)

④ **If** you're pregnant, you may be tempted to skip wearing a seat belt **as** you get bigger **because** it gets uncomfortable. **But** researchers from the University of Utah found **that** pregnant crash victims who didn't wear a seat belt were twice as likely to experience excessive maternal bleeding and nearly three times as likely to have their fetus die **than** belted moms-to-be involved in a crash. (**be tempted to do sth**: would like to do sth.)

⑤ In the section on bunker play, there is a discussion of the importance of raking over your footprints in the sand **after** you have played a shot. It is worth reiterating this point **because** there is scarcely a more depressing moment in a round **than** when you walk up to a bunker only to find your ball resting in a deep footprint. (**reiterate** (v): to repeat)

Unit 55 Conjunction *that*

GRAMMAR NOTES

(1) Functions of nominal *that*-clauses

- *That Jason lies* really bothers my mother. / *It* really bothers my mother *that Jason lies.*
- Margaret believes *that Charlie is honest.*
- Her hope is *that the exam will be easy.*
- The officer advised us *that the road was closed.*
- She made *it* obvious *that she didn't enjoy the food.*
- I welcome *the news that attacks on women on the railways are 19 percent down.*
- We were worried *that she was going to die*

(2) Verb complementation of *that*-clause

- They *agreed* that she *was* misled. (factual)
- People are *demanding* that he *leave / should leave / leaves* the company. (suasive)
- I *regret* that she *worries / should worry* about it. (emotive)
- It *surprises* me that he *worries / should worry* about it.

(3) Adjective complementation of *that*-clauses

- We were *confident* that Karen *was* still alive. (*aware, certain, confident, sure,* ···) (certainty - indicative verb)
- I am *anxious* that he *be / should be* permitted to resign. (*anxious, eager, willing,*···) (volition - subjunctive verb)
- I am *sorry* (that) you *have* to leave so early. / (that) you *should have* been (so) inconvenienced. (*angry, annoyed, glad, pleased, surprised,* ···)
  (emotion - putative *should*)
- I am *surprised* (that) you *didn't call* the doctor before. / (that) anyone of your intelligence *should swallow* a lie like that.

(4) Types of adjective in extraposed *that*-clause subject

- It is *true* that she *is* a vegetarian. (certainty - indicative verb)
- It is *essential* that the ban (*should*) *be / is* lifted tomorrow. (volition - subjunctive verb)
- It is *strange* that she *is / should be* so late. (emotion - putative *should*)

GRAMMATICAL EXPLORATION IN CONTEXT 

① **It** is my belief **that** the presence of students from all over the world enriches the quality of the educational experience that we offer. I therefore invite you to join us in Cambridge this summer.

② One of the first things you should know about chipping is **that** the way the ball behaves through the air and on the ground varies enormously from club to club.

③ "I **think** he will make a great public servant. I **think** he's got everything you would want in a politician. I **think** he's honest, I **think** he's charismatic and I **think** he's powerful. He has got a good family life and he's got a good history in that family of public service."

④ Gov. Pataki, facing **criticism that** he failed to maintain the state's grid, **contended** Tuesday **that** the system is not outdated and **that** there was no failure of New York's transmission system. (**contend** (v): to argue or maintain.)

⑤ It is regrettable, however, to **see that** in certain countries there attempts to restrict the freedom of opinion and expression on this issue. **It** should be remembered **that** there is no agreement among international scholars on the death tolls or the true nature of the tragic events that caused significant losses of life among Armenians and Turks during World War I.

Unit 56 Relative clauses

GRAMMAR NOTES

(1) Restrictive and non-restrictive relative clauses

- I have a friend *who plays guitar.*
- My father, *who retired last year*, now lives in Florida.
- Pat is *afraid of snakes*, *which* I'm sure Kim is too.
- *Pat is afraid of snakes*, *which* doesn't surprise me at all.
- The country was hit by 20 *storms* last year, *three of which* were super typhoons.

(2) *who, whom, that,* and no relative pronoun

(a) When we add information about people, we generally prefer *that* (or *no relative pronoun*) as object in informal contexts rather than *who* or *whom*:

- That's the man (*that*) I met at Alison's party.
- Our Squalene is 99.9% pure and extracted from liver oil of Aizame (dogfish) sharks, *who* inhabit non-polluted waters at depths of 3,000 feet.

(b) As with the interrogative pronouns, *who* is the normal form for the subjective and objective cases, whereas *whom* is used only in very formal and rarely used in spoken English:

- The boy (*that / no relative pronoun, who*) Elena had shouted at smiled.
- He is not the candidate *who* we voted for.

(c) When we add information about things in restrictive relative clauses, we can use *that* (or *no relative pronoun*) as object in conversation and *which* in more formal contexts:

- The dentist *that* you're seeing just lost his license.
- The curry (*that*) I cooked was too hot.

(d) We use *that* as subject after *something, anything, all, little, much, none,* and *superlatives. Which* is also used as subject after *something* and *anything*, but less commonly:

- These walls are *all that* remain of the city.
- "It's probably *the most difficult fire* we've fought in quite a while," Howe said.

GRAMMATICAL EXPLORATION IN CONTEXT 

① He walked slowly into the courthouse with his sister Janet, **who** is also a singer, arriving a total of 15 minutes late, **which** brought a sharp warning from Judge Rodney S. Melville of Santa Barbara County Superior Court.

② The Freedom From Smoking group clinic is a seven-week, eight-session program for people **that** want to quit smoking. Each participant will develop an individualized plan for quitting.

③ It is inspiring. Clinton does write movingly about people she met, places she visited and causes she supported in this country and around the globe in her eight years as first lady.

④ We had just finished a fancy dinner with my boss and his wife when my toddler unleashed a loud belch and attempted to unbuckle his pants. Horrified, I sternly told him to act like a big boy, **to which** he quickly replied, "I'm like Daddy." My husband usually unbuckles his pants after eating a large meal. Unfortunately, my boss and his wife were not amused.

(if you call a child **a big boy or a big girl**, you mean they are getting older and will soon be an adult: *Come on, you're a big girl now* (= old enough to behave like an adult)

⑤ A language so widely distributed naturally has many varieties. These are known as dialects. That word doesn't apply just to rural or uneducated forms of speech; the way we use it here, everyone speaks a dialect. And naturally, this book doesn't try to describe all the different dialects of English **there are**. It concentrates on one central dialect **that** is particularly important: the one **that** we call Standard English.

Unit 57 Discourse connectors

GRAMMAR NOTES

Discourse connectors join ideas between sentences or larger stretches of text and are frequently classified according to broad discourse-functional criteria; *additive, adversative, causal,* and *sequential.*

(1) **Additive**: involving new information

Emphatic: *in addition, moreover, furthermore, besides, also*

Appositional: *that is, in other words, for instance*

Comparative: *likewise, similarly*

- Smith probably committed the crime. He had a guilty look on his face. *Moreover,* the police found a gun under his bed.
- John Sudstrom wears only Ralph Lauren shirts. *Similarly,* his brother Fred buys only designer pants.

(2) **Adversative**: contrary to expectations

Proper adversative: *however, nevertheless, despite this, in contrast*

Contrastive: *in fact, actually, however, on the other hand, at the same time*

Correction: *instead, rather, on the contrary, at least*

Dismissal: *in any case, anyhow, at any rate*

- You could fly via Seattle; *however*, this isn't the only way.
- Minnesota is bitterly cold in the winter. *On the other hand*, it is one of the more scenic states.

(3) **Causal**: involving true causes and logical inferences

General causal: *therefore, consequently, for that reason, thus*

Causal conditional: *then, in that case, otherwise*

- There was no heating in the building. *As a result*, the workers had to be sent home.
- We could go skiing at Christmas. *Alternatively,* we could just stay at home.

(4) **Sequential**: concerning real-time relationships or sequential relationships; *then, next, first, second, last, finally, up to now, to sum up*

- *Up to now*, we've had very mild weather this winter.
- *Finally*, I'd like to thank everyone for coming this evening.
- *First*, I want to explain the purpose of this meeting.

GRAMMATICAL EXPLORATION IN CONTEXT 

① A reading room in the Food Science Building offers journals and books. **In addition,** students may avail themselves of books, journals, and reprints owned by faculty members.

② Workers began repairing the building's exterior early this year. In two years, the cottage will be open to the public as a museum. **Meanwhile**, you can glimpse the Lincoln Cottage from the outside on special summer bus tours. (**meanwhile** (adv): from now until a time or event in the future)

③ Every state has toughened driver's license procedures since the 2001 attacks. Many have added safeguards **such as** watermarks, fingerprints and digital photographs.
(**toughen / toughen up**: become more strict or make something more strict, *Universities are toughening up their entrance requirements.* **watermark** (n): a hidden design on a piece of paper that you can only see when you hold the paper up near a light.)

④ After 20 years of practicing pediatrics, I'm still astonished by the miracle of the newborn child. Amazingly, the majority of little ones come into the world perfectly healthy. **Yet** I seldom meet an expectant parent who isn't concerned about the possibility of a birth defect.
(**expectant** (adj): (*only before noun*) an expectant parent will soon be a parent of a new baby)

⑤ Such differences between the two channels affect our language use in several ways. One is that spoken communication requires fast, almost instantaneous production and understanding. **On the other hand**, when we write, we usually have time to revise, check and rewrite what we have written. **Likewise**, when we receive a piece of writing we can read it, reread it, ponder over it, and discuss it. (**instantaneous** (adj): immediate, instant)

Unit 58 Postmodifications

GRAMMAR NOTES

Types of postmodifiers

(1) Relative clauses

- They read every book *that they could borrow in the village.*

(2) Non-finite clauses

(a) ~*ing* participle clauses

- People *working in the IT business* are often young.
- Last Friday I got a letter *saying that there was trouble afoot.*

(b) ~*ed* participle clauses

- The question *debated in Parliament yesterday* was about the new tax.
- We have seen the damage to the pine *done by the deer.*

(c) *to*-infinitive clauses

- The next plane *to arrive* was from Manila.
- Mr. Knowles is the last person *to cause trouble.*

(3) Prepositional phrases

- The world has to reduce its output *of greenhouse gases.*
- We've rented this cottage *in the country* for peace and quiet.

(4) Appositive clauses

- There is no getting away from the fact *that inflation is causing hardship.*
- It is reported that there has been a plot *to overthrow the government.*

(5) Adjectives

- There's nothing *new* about these techniques.
- All the persons *present* at the meeting were in favor of the proposal.

(6) Adverbs

- Where's the way *out*?
- Can you find the road *back*?

(7) Clauses of time, place, manner and reason

- Can you give me a time *when you will be free*?
- In Stratford-on-Avon we visited the house *where Shakespeare lived.*
- The way (*that*) *you suggested to solve the problem* didn't work.
- Is there any reason *to believe that she isn't telling the truth*?

GRAMMATICAL EXPLORATION IN CONTEXT 

① "Another great job guys. Aside from having a great product, your site allows a lefty **like myself** to purchase the clubs **that I need** with the options and upgrades **that I want.**"

② The forty-four attorneys **involved in the impeachment inquiry** worked seven days a week, barricaded in the old Congressional Hotel on Capitol Hill. I was twenty-six years old, awed by the company **I was keeping** and the historic responsibility **we had assumed.** (**the company sb keeps**: the people that someone spends time with)

③ I represent the most diverse, exciting, dynamic state in the most diverse, exciting, dynamic nation in the world. And every day **that I go to the floor of the United States Senate**, I'm profoundly moved by that privilege and humbled by the responsibility **I have been given by the people of New York.**

④ Just hours after the administration's much-awaited report reached Capitol Hill, the House responded by approving legislation **requiring U.S. combat forces to start leaving Iraq within 120 days**. The resolution passed on a largely party-line vote, with only four Republican defections – a reflection **of White House efforts to keep House Republicans from joining restive GOP senators** in challenging the president.

⑤ Coming soon – later this year – and perhaps to an airport near you: **very light jets, the latest category in business aviation.** VLJs are business jets **that weigh less than 10,000 pounds, or 4.5 metric tons**. Typically they are small twin-engine planes **designed to carry six or eight people, including crew, on short-haul flights of about 600 to 1,200 miles, or 1,000 to 2,000 kilometers – the distance between, for example, Berlin and Istanbul or between Shanghai and Manila.**

Unit 59 Reporting

GRAMMAR NOTES

(1) Quoting and reporting in our own words

More commonly, especially in speech, we report in our own words what people think or what they have said.

(*reporting clause*)	(*reported clause*)
She explained	(that) she couldn't take the job until January.
He didn't ask me	where to put the boxes.

- "When will you be back?" *asked Arnold.*
- I *don't* expect he will come. (transferred negation)
  (*believe, feel, intend, plan, propose, suppose, think, want*)
- "What's the problem?" → She asked me *what* the problem was.
- "Have you seen Paul recently?"
  → She wanted to know if / whether I had seen Paul recently.

(2) The uses of reporting verbs

- I *notified the bank that* I had changed my address. (*assure, convince, inform, notify, persuade, reassure, remind, tell, warn,* …)
- *We have been informed that* we have to leave the building.
- They *promised* (*me*) *that* they would come to the party. (*advise, promise, show, teach, warn,* …)
- She *admitted* (*to me*) *that* she was seriously ill. (*announce, complain, confess, explain, indicate, mention, propose, recommend, report, say, suggest,* …)
- We *agreed* (*with Susan*) *that* the information should go no further. (*argue, check, disagree, joke,* …)
- The company *demands* (*of its staff*) *that* they should be at work by 8.30.
  (*ask, demand, require,* …)
- I felt that the results were satisfactory. → I felt the results to be satisfactory. (*acknowledge, assume, believe, consider, expect, find, presume, report, think, understand,* …)
- *It is reported that* the damage is extensive.
  → The damage is reported to be extensive.
- It is thought that there are too many obstacles to peace.
  → There are thought to be too many obstacles to peace.

GRAMMATICAL EXPLORATION IN CONTEXT

① In recent years, the Department of Agriculture has been **warned** numerous times **that** its testing system was not going to be able to stop mad cow disease from getting into American beef.

② "When Callaway Golf **told** me that they had a new ball for me to try, the first question that I asked them was if it was better than my original HX ball. They **told** me to go out and try it for myself. Now I can't imagine hitting anything else. It's incredibly fast off the clubface, but it's also really responsive around the green. With the new HX Tour you literally get the best of both worlds – great control and great distance. What more could you possibly want from a golf ball?"

③ "Mr. Jackson, you have started out on the wrong foot with me," Judge Melville **said**. "I want to **advise** you that I will not put up with that. It's an insult to the court. You must be on time."
"Do you understand that?" the judge **asked** Mr. Jackson, who **replied** in a whisper, "Yes, sir."
(**start out** (get off / start off) **on the wrong** (right) **foot**; to immediately establish a bad (good) relationship with someone when you first meet them or first start working with them: *I got off on the wrong foot with Patrick.* **put up with**: endure, tolerate)

④ On Mount Washington in New Hampshire today, the observatory **reported** that temperatures of 39 degrees below zero **felt** like minus 87 degrees because of powerful wind gusts of up to 103 miles per hour.

⑤ Snow **is expected to** begin late this afternoon or by early this evening, continuing tonight and ending Thursday morning. This storm **is expected to** be of only moderate intensity as well as move quickly through the area.

Unit 60 Tense choice in reporting

GRAMMAR NOTES

- "I'm leaving." → Bob *announced* that he *was* leaving.
- "Are you going to London?" → Mark *asked* me if I *was going* to London.
- "We have found the missing girl." → Last night police *said* that they *had found* the missing girl.
- Officials *said* the possibility of sanctions *would* be part of a broader diplomatic campaign intended to get North Korea to step back from its nuclear programs.

(1) Clear context that one event took place before another

- "I've sent out the invitations. I did it well before the wedding." → She *reassured* me that she *sent* (*had sent*) out the invitations well before the wedding.

(2) Present tense (reporting clause) → present tense (reported clause):

permanent / habitual or still existing or relevant situation

- Dr Weir *thinks* that he *spends* about 5 minutes on a typical appointment with a patient.
- US scientists *claim* that they *have developed* a new vaccine against malaria.

(3) Past tense (reporting clause) → present or past tense (reported clause)

Choosing a present tense (or present perfect) in the reported clause emphasizes that the situation being reported *still exists or is still relevant* when we report it.

- She *argued* that Carl *is / was* the best person for the job.
- Sarah *told* me that she *has / had* two houses.
- Forecasters tracking the hurricane's likely path *predicted* Isabel *will* barrel into the Outer Banks of North Carolina by about noon ET Thursday.

GRAMMATICAL EXPLORATION IN CONTEXT 

① He **told** the Commons there **was** still time for Iraq to avoid a war, but if the peaceful route **was** rejected, the country **would** be disarmed by force.
(**the Commons**: the House of the Commons (U.K) / the House of the Representatives (U.S))

② The United States **said** it **wanted** a diplomatic solution, but there **were** fears that if the U.S. **took** military action, it **would** damage China's economic stability, especially if Pyongyang **allowed** a flood of refugees to cross its border with China.
(**flood** (n): a large number of people or things that move somewhere or arrive somewhere at the same time: *We received a flood of letters protesting against the change.*)

③ Mohammed Aldouri, Iraq's ambassador to the U.N., said he took comfort from the inspectors' reports and **repeated** Iraq's claims that it no longer **possesses** weapons of mass destruction. "An empty hand has nothing to give," he said.
(**comfort** (n): a feeling of being less sad, or worried about something than you were previously. **take comfort from sth**: *I take comfort from the fact his friends are there to help him.*)

④ Susan E. Rice, a Brookings Institution scholar and former assistant secretary of state for African affairs in the Clinton administration, **said** the White House **is not spending** as much money as it says, but added, "I have to say this is much better than I might have feared."

⑤ Two administration officials **said** Bush **plans** to announce additional aid to Africa at the G8 summit on top of the $674 million in new assistance he announced at this week's White House meeting with Blair. (**on top of**: in addition to something else: *On top of all his financial problems, his wife left him.*)

Unit 61 Focus and emphasis

GRAMMAR NOTES

(1) Phonological form
- John cooked the *DINNER.* / *JOHN* cooked the dinner.
/ John *COOKED* the dinner.

(2) Morphological and lexical devices
(a) Repetition
- This house is *far, far* too expensive.
- I think that the lecturers are *very, very* boring.

(b) Emphatic DO
- You *do* look pretty. - What *did* happen? - *Do* come early.
- My teacher claims that I didn't turn in my paper but I *did* turn it in.

(c) Emphatic reflexive pronouns
- The victims *themselves* can't explain how the accident occurred.
- I saw the president *himself.* - I saw the president *myself.*

(d) Emphatic *own*
- He spent only his *own* money. - Is that Johnny's very *own* BMW?

(e) Emphatic adjectives and adverbs
- an *outright* lie * This lie is outright. - a *mere* child *The child is mere.
- We are *utterly* powerless.

(3) Syntactic means
(a) Marked word order
- *Him* I like; *her* I don't. (I like *him* but I don't (like) *her.*)
- *Ambitious* she must have been, or she wouldn't have come.
- *A professor* he was, but in name only.
- *Not* a penny of the money did he spend.
- *Never* have I seen such a mess!
- *So* absurd was his manner *that* everyone laughed at him.
- Even more *roguish* was John's younger brother.
- *Sitting* at the kitchen table was our missing uncle.
- *At the kitchen table* was our missing uncle.

(b) Special focus constructions
- I don't mind her criticizing me, but *it's* how she does it *that* I object to.
- *What she is is* a brilliant reporter.

GRAMMATICAL EXPLORATION IN CONTEXT

① If you **do** smoke, find an open area away from your family - but know that your baby can still absorb nicotine through your hair and clothing, etc. And **never** smoke while breast-feeding. Nicotine passes through a mother's milk to her baby.

② You should use the same amount of acceleration in your downswing for all three shots: **it is** the length of your backswing **that** determines how far the ball will travel.

③ David lost his job and was short of money, so **what he did was (to) sell** his flat and move in with his brother.
(**move in with**: to start living in the same place as someone else)

④ For years afterwards, the scenes I witnessed at Huairou remained etched in my mind. **Seldom does one see so tangibly**, in one setting, the differences between living in a free society and living under government control.

⑤ Subhash owed 40,000 rupees, or $890, to the bank, and about 100,000 rupees more to private lenders in the village - with no way of repaying the loans. "I could see that he was worried, but I had no idea he would commit suicide," she (Subhash's widow) said. One of the guests, Kishar Sikkalwar, the leader of a neighboring village, spoke more angrily. "He should have told us about his problems, and not done such a foolish thing," he said. It is not clear that Sikkalwar would have been able to offer much help. He **himself** owes the bank about 100, 000 rupees, which he cannot repay because of crop failure. Plunging the wedding party into a deeper desolation, he rattled off the names of seven farmers he knew who have killed **themselves** this season as a result of the poor harvest.

Unit 62 Cleft sentences

GRAMMAR NOTES

(1) *It*-clefts

An *it*-cleft is a specially marked construction that puts some constituent, typically an NP, into focus. The construction implies contrast.

- The manager mows the lawn.
  → It's the manager who mows the lawn (not a gardener).
- It's not the gardener who mows the lawn (but the manager).
- It's not the gardener, but the manager, who mows the lawn.
- John wants a car. → It's a car that John wants (not a house).
- It's in the kitchen that I study (not in the den).
- It was because he was jealous that Bobby lied about his sister's prize (not for some other reason).
- "Who cleans the house – the man or the woman?" "It's the woman that / who cleans the house." (*it*-cleft)
  cf. "Who's that?" "It's the woman *that / who* clean the house. (relative clause)

(2) *Wh*-clefts

Wh-clefts or 'pseudo clefts' are the other important focus construction in English. *Wh*-clefts can be reversed, although they occur primarily in initial position.

- What he is, is a complete fool. / A complete fool is what he is.
- We need more time → It's more time that we need. (*it*-cleft)
  → What we need is more time. (*wh*-cleft)
  → We don't need more money – what we need is more time. (contrast)

(3) Comparison of *it*-cleft and *wh*-cleft sentences

The focus of the *wh*-cleft normally has to be in the form of a noun phrase or nominal clause. An adverbial phrase or prepositional phrase sounds less natural in *wh*-cleft but somewhat better when *wh*-cleft comes last.

- It was *on this very spot* that I first met my wife.
  cf. On this very spot was *where I first met my wife.*
- It is *in the autumn* that the countryside is most beautiful.
  cf. (In) Autumn is *when the countryside is most beautiful.*

GRAMMATICAL EXPLORATION IN CONTEXT 

① Ballack insists **it is** for the challenge, not the money, but it is no shock **that** he moves to Chelsea, which made him an offer with which Bayern cannot compete.

② "I've herd various comments," Christensen said. "But **what's clear to me is** this boat wouldn't have happened without this crew. I think you could have picked all the other teams here and put them with this project, and you wouldn't have ended up with this boat."

③ In a reference to the United States, he harshly criticized "diktat and imperialism" in global affairs and warned that Russia will keep strengthening its military potential to maintain a global strategic balance. "**It** wasn't us **who** initiated a new round of arms race," Putin said when asked about Russia's missile tests this week at a news conference after talks in the Kremlin with Greek President Karolos Papoulias.

④ The voices of this conference and of the women at Huairou must be heard loud and clear: **It** is a violation of human rights **when** babies are denied food, or drowned, or suffocated, or their spines broken, simply because they are born girls. **It** is a violation of human rights **when** women and girls are sold into the slavery of prostitution.

⑤ Outside the hall, women hung over banisters and rushed down escalators to grab my hand. I was thrilled that my message had resonated, and **it** was a relief **that** the press reports, too, were good. The New York Times editorial page wrote that the speech "may have been her finest moment in public life." **What** I didn't know at the time **was that** my twenty-one-minute speech would become a manifesto for women all over the world.

Unit 63 *There* constructions

GRAMMAR NOTES

(1) *There* + *be* + indefinite NP (+ place or time position adverbial)
- *There's* a lot of noise here. (existential *there*)
  cf. *There* are your friends. (deictic *there*)
- There's *a little boy* who looks after the sheep. (existential *there*)
  cf. There's *the little boy* who looks after the sheep. (*deictic* there)
- *There* were a lot of events that happened in my country.
- *There* are thought to be too many obstacles to peace.

(2) *There's* before a plural noun in *informal* speech
- 'Anything to eat?' 'Well, *there's* some apples on the table.'
- Well, it's not all fun. *There's* long hikes in the mud and rain.
- *There's* so many things to talk about.

(3) Verbs other than *be* with *there* constructions
(a) verbs of existence: *arise, dwell, emerge, exist, lie, live, remain, stand,* (b) event verbs that describe something happening, … : *appear, arise, develop, emerge, happen, occur,* … (c) verbs of motion or direction: *approach, come, fly, go, run, walk,* …
- I can't contact Tim. There *must be* something wrong with his phone.
- There *may* come a time when we will meet.
- There *appears to be* a major disagreement between the two presidents.
- There *developed* a problem in the ignition.
- There *seems* to have been some carelessness.

(4) *There* + *be* + noun + *that–, wh–, to–*infinitive or *~ing* clause:
- Is there a chance (*that*) Lee could arrive this afternoon?
- There is no reason (*why*) I can't see you tomorrow.
- There is a small stream *that* runs at the bottom of the garden.
- There was an attempt *to resolve* the dispute at the factory.
- There was a taxi *waiting* outside the hotel.
- *There being* no evidence against him, he was released. (formal)

(5) *There* + *be* + *the* / *that–*: to show a change of topic or the topic already known to the listener or reader
- … And then *there is the* question of who is going to pay.
- *There never was that* problem in Austin. (anaphoric *that*)

GRAMMATICAL EXPLORATION IN CONTEXT

① I decided to visit Kossar's on my return to the subway, and did. **There was** only one man behind the counter, and I was the only customer. **There were** some delicious-looking long rolls in the window that were not familiar to me. I asked him what they were and he replied, "Bulkas."

② **There has been a lot of talk** in Washington about refashioning Iraq into a prosperous, tolerant democracy that can serve as a model for the Middle East. Unfortunately, **there hasn't been much plain speaking** about how much that is going to cost.

(**plain** (adj): expressing what you think honestly, using simple, direct language: *a plain answer*. **plain speaking / talking**: She was admired for her plain speaking.)

③ Your baby's soft, beautiful skin is probably a pleasure to caress and squeeze. And then **there's that heavenly scent** ··· But beautiful baby skin can develop blotches and spots.

(**caress** (v): to move your hands gently over someone's face or body in a way that shows you love them.)

④ "When people say **there are** no oceans or lakes, does that mean **there was no life**? Not at all," he said. **"There's the possibility** that ice and snow on Mars melted from time to time, forming those gullies and then refreezing again."

⑤ *There*, to the left, is *the* perfectly manicured golf course, an island of green erupting from the desert. *Here,* to the right, are two of the spotless tennis courts. **There are** six in all. He points out the five pools, the hot tubs, the corral for horses, the hiking trails leading into the mountains. **There's** even a fishing lake stocked with catfish.

Unit 64 Negation

GRAMMAR NOTES

(1) The negation system: its forms

(a) At the word or lexical level, one can simply use a negative affix in English to convey negativity. The way to make many adjectives and adverbs negative is to add a negative derivational prefix to a word:

happy – *un*happy, appropriate – *in*appropriate, possible - *im*possible
logical – *il*logical, relevant – *ir*relevant, ordered – *dis*ordered
typical - *a*typical

(b) At the phrase level, *no* can function as a negative determiner in a noun phrase. Before infinitive verbs in infinitive phrases, *not* is used to make the phrase negative

- I am surprised that *no* alternative was proposed.
- *No* plans have been made.
- Marge has decided *not* to pay her income tax this year.

(c) *Not* is the main sentence-level negator. However, *no* can also make a sentence negative, especially when it negates the subject.

- John is *not* at home.
- *No* one was home to sign for the package.
- He is *not able* to do it, *is she*?
  cf. He is *unable* to do it, *isn't she*?

(2) The scope of negation

- Joe obviously *hasn't* understood a word. (= It is obvious that he did not.)
- Joe *hasn't* obviously understood a word. (= It is not obvious that he did)
- I did*n't* attend *any* of the lectures. (= I attended none of the lectures.)
- I did*n't* attend *some* of the lectures. (= There are some lectures that I didn't attend.)

GRAMMATICAL EXPLORATION IN CONTEXT

① But **what few of them knew** was that when Mastanduno fulfilled his dream – he was sworn in last night as a Woodbridge firefighter – he would fulfill a promise: asking Yoon to marry him.
(**swear in** (v): to make someone give a formal promise in a law court or at an official ceremony: *He was sworn in as president.*)

② "I think people use 'stress' more than they are comfortable saying 'mental health,' because **fewer people** are able to admit to having problems with mental health," Knapp said.

③ The following drills are a few of the ones that I use for beginner golfers and they would**n't** hurt veteran golfers **either**.

④ There are many reasons for legs to ache at the end of the day. Often it's simply because of an increased amount of standing or even doing too much exercise. But your story doesn't indicate any recent increase in **either**.

⑤ But when my work is complete I'll go to New York to meet my girlfriend. We **won't** be going to a vigil or memorial, **nor** to discuss how we've changed since Sept. 10, 2001, but simply to enjoy a dinner one September night. Hopefully others will be able to do the same, even after "everything changed." (**vigil** (n): a period of time at night when you stay awake to pray)

Unit 65 Inversion

GRAMMAR NOTES

(1) Inversion **after adverbial phrases of direction, place, and time**
- Here *comes the first question.*
- Beside the barn *stand a silo* and several tractors.
- Then *came the turning point of the match.*
- Next *came the Chaplain.*

(2) Inversion **in conditional sentences**
- It would be a serious setback, *were the talks* to fail.
- *Should you* need more information, please telephone our main office.
- *Had they* not rushed Dan to hospital, he would have died.

(3) Inversion **in comparisons with '*as*' and '*than*'**
- The cake was excellent, as *was the coffee.*
- Oil costs less than *would atomic energy.*

(4) Inversion **after negative adverbials**
- Seldom *do we* have goods returned to us because they are faulty.
- Not since Sept. 11, 2001, *has President Bush* faced a test quite like the one he confronts now.
- Only when he came closer *did she* realize he was a stranger.

(5) Inversion **after '*so* + *adj* ··· *that*', '*such* + *be* ··· *that*', '*neither* / *nor* ···'**
- So dangerous *did weather conditions* become, that all mountain roads were closed.
- If you will not do so, neither *will I.*
- She hadn't known much about life, nor *had he.*

(6) Inversion is found only if the negative scope affects the whole of the clause. Thus there is **no inversion** in:
- *No doubt* she'll tell me everything when she's ready.
- *In no time* they had defeated the enemy.
- *Not long ago* there was a rainstorm somewhere in the valley.
- *Only* those who receive an invitation are invited.

(7) When an object is placed in initial position, there is **no inversion.**
- Why didn't you tell me? Such things *you must* tell me.
- Some things *you forget*, Other things *you never do.*
- What they can do, *we can do.*

GRAMMATICAL EXPLORATION IN CONTEXT

① Today is Veterans Day, a federal, state and local holiday in New Jersey and New York. **Here is a list** of closings and transit schedules for today: Federal offices and courts are closed. Post offices are closed. There is no regular mail delivery, except for Express Mail and special delivery. (**Veterans Day** = Veteran's Day, **transit** (n): transportation)

② The Pocono Mountains of Northeastern Pennsylvania, USA offer 2,400 square miles of wooded peaks and valleys with numerous sparkling lakes, rushing rivers, and some of the loveliest waterfalls anywhere. In the midst of such natural beauty **are some of the most superb golf resorts** and golf courses in the state of Pennsylvania.

③ On the first day of October, Physical Fitness Center will be re-opened to all its members with additional new programs and the amended schedule for all of them. Your employees are our most frequent visitors to the center. Attached **is the revised schedule** in our Center. Also **included is a new feature** that will surely attract your employees.

④ The history books of the 20th century are full of the names of dictators who killed millions. **Less well known is the name of one man** credited with saving more lives than anyone who has ever lived by keeping tens of millions from starving in the 1960s.
(**credit sb with sth**: (*often passive*) to say or believe that someone is responsible for a particular achievement: *Clinton credited Mike Boorda with bringing peace to Bosnia.*)

⑤ "There are no winners. We are all losers," Blah said in his inaugural address. "We are all one people irrespective of tribe, religious beliefs and political beliefs. **No more shall we** fight amongst ourselves."

Unit 66 Ellipsis

GRAMMAR NOTES

(1) Textual ellipsis

- Peter ate the apple and (Peter/he) drank the beer.
- Peter must have broken in and (Peter must have) stolen the papers.
- Peter will be playing the guitar and Mary (will be) preparing supper.
- His sister has always been more athletic than *he.*
- Willie likes Lily more than *she* (likes Lily).
- Willie likes Lily more than (he likes) *her.*
- All the people we had invited turned up, and some that we had not invited (turned up)

(2) Situational ellipsis

- *Love* you so much. / *Hope* she's coming.
- You a smoker? / You okay?
- Where you *been*?
- *Working* late, Mr. Johnson.
- (I am) Much obliged (= Thank you very much)
- *Selling* this car?
- Anybody home?
- So many places to go and so many things to do.
- *Mind* if I ask you a question? / *Need* any help? / a cart? / Want a drink?
- Why pay more?
- *Better* be careful.
- You *better* check it before you buy it. (spoken/informal)
- *Got* something to say? / *Been* married long? / *Been* busy? */Lost your cellphone*?
- *Not done* with your back to school shopping yet?
- (That) *Sounds* fine to me.
- Keep tube capped *when not in use.*
- In total, at least 52 people were killed and about 700 *wounded.*
- A glass of water.
  (Give me/ I want / I'll have / I'd like / Do you have / Can you give me / Could you give me)

GRAMMATICAL EXPLORATION IN CONTEXT

① Have you had your bone density checked lately? **If not, you should**. It's a quick and easy way to find out the strength of your bones.

② In the following pages you will find the most comprehensive list of the region's public golf courses available anywhere. This magazine is full of other useful information, as well. **Looking** for a neighborhood golf store? It's in here. **Looking** for a place to take your spring golf trip? We've got some suggestions.

③ The roof constitutes as much as 50 percent of a house's exterior, yet most homeowners don't give it a thought - until it leaks. **Why wait for problems?** The older your home is, the more vulnerable it is to harsh weather.
(**harsh** climates or conditions are very difficult for people, animals, and plants to live in: *The weather grew harsh, chilly and unpredictable.*)

④ For the third straight week, oil prices **were jacked up** by 50 pesos per liter and liquefied petroleum gas also by 50 pesos per kilogram.
(**jack up**: to increase the price, rate, or number of something by a large amount)

⑤ "But you do not realize that you are wretched, pitiful, poor, blind and naked. I counsel you to buy from me **gold** refined in the fire, so you can become rich; **white clothes** to wear, so you can cover your shameful nakedness; and **salve** to put on your eyes, so you can see.
(**counsel**: advise, **salve**: a medical cream that you spread on sore skin to reduce the pain.)

Unit 67 Parallel structures

GRAMMAR NOTES

(1) The term **parallel structure** (also called **parallelism**) is an important feature of English that makes our speaking, and especially our writing easier to understand. To make speech or writing parallel, similar ideas should be expressed in similar grammatical structures.

- *Early to bed and early to rise* make a man *healthy, wealthy,* and *wise.*
- The children *ran down the hill, skipped over the lawn,* and *jumped into the swimming pool.*
- *Living on your own* is a lot different from *living with your parents.*
- Children in this program are not allowed *to watch television* or *to eat junk food.*
- Being fired from his job made Tim *bitter, angry,* and *pessimistic.*
- *The sooner you decide, the better it will be*
- (If you do) *no work*, (you get) *no pay.*
- *Spare the rod*, and *spoil the child.*
- *In London I was born* and *in London I shall die.*
- *From the ceiling hung a huge lamp. Along the wall were pikes.*
- It was criticized *by some for being too short, by others for being too long.*
- We persuaded *one of them to cycle* and *the others to catch a bus.*
- Ted considered *Kim too young* and *Pat too earnest.*
- I sent *Ed a letter on Monday* and *Sue a postcard on Friday.*
- Kitchen rules: (1) *Coffee to be made* only by library staff. (2) *Coffee service to be closed* at 4:00 p.m. (3) *Coffee materials not to be handled* by faculty members.

(2) **Correlative conjunctions** (*both … and, either … or, neither … nor, not only … but also*) occur in pairs, which are usually used to compare two ideas.

- I must go home *either* today *or* tomorrow.
- He got an 'A' *not only* in math *but also* in English.
- She is *neither* a good housekeeper *nor* a good cook.
- She plays *both* the piano *and* the violin.
- We want you *neither* to stop studying *nor* to stop your sports activities.

GRAMMATICAL EXPLORATION IN CONTEXT

① The air base has played a central role **in** rooting out fighters of the Taliban and Al Qaeda and **in** carrying out relief operations.

② Each new baby is precious and unique. Being a parent is all about **getting** to know your child and **helping** this new little person grow up happy, healthy and ready to learn.

③ Our goals are **to maintain** New Jersey's rich variety of fish and wildlife species at stable, healthy levels and **to protect and enhance** the many habitats on which they depend.

④ The government, through a funding assistance from the United Nations Children's Fund (UNICEF), has launched a nationwide campaign, dubbed "Iwas Bird Flu," **to rally** the whole country in preventing the entry of the virus into the Philippines and **to be** prepared for any potential bird flu incidence.

⑤ India could obtain nuclear fuel and reactor components from the United States and other countries, and in return would allow international inspections and safeguards on its civilian nuclear program, and refrain **from** further weapons tests and **from** transferring arms technology to other countries.

Unit 68 Information structures

GRAMMAR NOTES

(1) Given and new information

We can roughly divide the information in a message into *given* information and *new* information:

Given information: something which the speaker assumes the hearer known about already

New information: something which the speaker does not assume the hearer knows about already.

A: What did she say to Kath?
B: She was speaking to me (not to Kath).
GIVEN NEW

Notice that given information and new information are what the speaker *presents* as given and new respectively. What *in fact* the hearer knows or assumes may be a different thing:

A: Do you like Picasso?
B: No, I hate modern painting.
NEW GIVEN

(Speaker B takes it *given* that Picasso is a modern painter)

(2) **Given information** is not just information which has already been mentioned or suggested. We may extend this notion to include information which is 'given' by the situation outside language. In this respect, 'given' information is like definite meaning and there is indeed a strong connection between given information and definiteness.

- What are you doing today?
NEW GIVEN
- What are you doing on Saturday?
NEW

(3) The principles of end-focus and end-weight

When deciding in which order to place the ideas in a sentence, there are two principles to remember:

(a) End-focus: The new or most important idea or message in a piece of information should be placed towards the end, where in speech the nucleus of the tone unit normally falls. In <writing> and prepared <speech>, this principle can be applied not just to a single piece of information, but to a whole sentence containing many pieces of information.

(b) End-weight: The more 'weighty' part(s) of a sentence should be placed towards the end. Otherwise the sentence may sound awkward and unbalanced. The 'weight' of an element can be defined in terms of its length (i.e. the number of its syllables or words).

- Sue picked up *the dog.* / Sue picked *the dog* up.
- Sue picked up *a couple of boxes containing old computer manuals.* / ?Sue picked *a couple of boxes containing old computer manuals* up.

- *Inside the house Mr. Summers* found a family of cats shut in the bathroom.
- *She is being treated* in hospital.
- Two letters have arrived for Jill; *she*'ll be calling round to pick *them* up.
- *I* haven't heard from Jill for a long time – have *you*? As a child, I used to pretend a unicorn lived in my backyard. I called *him* Joe.
- In the center, around the throne, were four living creatures, and *they* were covered with eyes, in front and in back.
- "What did Max tell Jill?" "*He told her* I'd been delayed at the office."
- The three machines tested for the report contained different types of safety valve. *All the equipment* was manufactured by the Boron Group in Germany. (all the equipment = topic / given)
- I don't in general care for puzzles, but *crossword puzzles* are fun.
- That book is awful; *the author* doesn't have any writing ability at all.
- I walked into the kitchen. On *a stool* was a large book.
- *The president* is giving the State of the Union address later tonight.

GRAMMATICAL EXPLORATION IN CONTEXT

① The officials said **the man** emerged from the same South London apartment complex as a prime suspect in the failed bombings of three subway trains and a double-decker bus, and **was followed** by armed plainclothes officers to a nearby subway station.

② The changing colors of autumn signal that **the trees** are getting ready for winter. Throughout the spring and summer most of the foods necessary for **the tree's growth** are made in the leaves. This food-making process takes place in the cells containing chlorophyll, which gives leaves their green color.

③ Pennsylvania boasts one of the largest systems of state parks and state forests in the country. Covering nearly 2.4 million acres, **these public lands are carefully conserved** to provide access to scenic beauty, natural treasures, learning experiences and countless recreational opportunities.

④ This major international energy conference, now in its 27th year, will be addressed by oil ministers from the world's largest producing nations and senior oil industry executives. **Among the topics under discussion will be: (1) Human resource constraints – How serious and how lasting?** (2) Energy security risks: European natural gas …

⑤ In 1991, two thieves stole 20 paintings form this museum, valued at $10 million each. **The loot** included Van Gogh's most celebrated work, "Sunflowers." Amazingly, **the works** were recovered hours later when police found them in the thieves' getaway car, but **the burglars** were long gone. Chances are they had difficulty selling the paintings and decided to give them up rather than risk getting caught by trying to sell them.

Bibliography

Alexander, L. G. 1990. *Longman English Grammar Practice*. London: Longman

Azar, B. S. 1989. *Understanding and Using English Grammar*. Englewood Cliffs, New Jersey: Prentice-Hall Regents

______. 1992. *Fundamentals of English Grammar*. Englewood Cliffs, New Jersey: Prentice-Hall Regents

Azar, B. S. and D. A. Azar 1992. *Understanding and Using English Grammar, workbook*. Englewood Cliffs, New Jersey: Prentice-Hall Regents

Ball, W. J. 1989. *Dictionary of Link Words*. Macmillan Publishers Ltd

Biber, D., S. Johansson, G. Leech, S, Conrad, and E. Finegan. 1999. *Longman Grammar of Spoken and Written English*. London: Longman

Bolinger, D. 1961. 'Contrastive Accent and Contrastive Stress.' *Language 37*, 83-96.

______. 1971a. 'A further note on the nominal in the progressive.' *Linguistic Inquiry I*, 584-586

______. 1971b. *The Phrasal Verb in English. Cambridge*, Mass: Harvard University Press

______. 1972. *Degree Words*. The Hague: Mouton

______. 1977. *Meaning and form*. London: Longman

______. 1979. 'Pronouns in Discourse.' *Syntax and Semantics 12*, 289-309.

Close, R. A. 1974. *A University Grammar of English, workbook*. London: Longman

Cobuild English Dictionary. 1995. London: Harper Collins Publishers

Cobuild Student's Grammar. 1991. London: Harper Collins Publishers

Comrie, B. 1976. *Aspect*. Cambridge University Press

Fuchs, M., M. Westheimer, M. Bonner. 1994. *Focus on Grammar: An Intermediate Course for Reference and Practice*, vol. A & B, London: Longman

Givón, T. 1979a. *On Understanding Grammar*. New York: Academic Press

______ ed. 1979b. *Syntax and Semantics 12 : discourse and syntax*. New York: Academic Press.

______. 1993. *English Grammar - A function-based Introduction*. Amsterdam: J. Benjamins

Grice, Paul. 1989. *Studies in the Way of Words*. Harvard University Press.

Halliday, M. A. K. and R. Hasan. 1976. *Cohesion in English*. London: Longman

Hawkins, J. A. 1978. *Definiteness and Indefiniteness*. London: Croom Helm

Hewings, M. 2005. *Advanced Grammar in Use*. Cambridge University press.

Huddleston, R. 1988. *English Grammar: an outline*. Cambridge University Press

Jespersen, O. 1933. *Essentials of English Grammar*. London: Allen and Unwin

______. 1951. *The Philosophy of Grammar*. London: Allen and Unwin

Jones, L. 1992. *Communicative Grammar Practice*. Cambridge University Press

Jun, C. B. 2001. *A Practical University Grammar of English*. Pusan: Ilo Publishing Co.

Kilby, D. 1984. *Descriptive Syntax and the English Verb*. London: Croom Helm

Koch, R. S. 1995. *Focus on Grammar, workbook: An Advanced Course for Reference and Practice*. London: Longman

Kuno, S. 1987. *Functional Syntax*. University of Chicago Press

Leech, G. and J. Svartvik 2002. *A Communicative Grammar of English*. 3rd ed. London: Longman

Li, C. N. 1976. (ed) *Subject and Topic*. New York: Academic Press

Long, R. 1961. *The Sentence and its Parts: A Grammar of Contemporary English. Chicago*: University of Chicago Press

Longman Dictionary of Contemporary English. 1978. London: Longman

Longman Dictionary of English Idioms. 1979. London: Longman

Macmillan English Dictionary for advanced learners of American English. 2002. Macmillan Publishers Ltd.

Maurer, J. 1995. *Focus on Grammar: An Advanced Course for Reference and Practice*. London: Longman

Murphy, R. 1989. *Grammar in Use: Reference and Practice for Intermediate Students of English.* Cambridge University Press

_____. 1994. *English Grammar in Use: A Self-study Reference and Practice for Intermediate Students*. Cambridge University Press

Palmer, F. R. 1974. *The English Verb*. London: Longman

Perlmutter, D. M. 1970. *On the Article in English*. The Hague: Mouton

Prince. E. 1978. 'A comparison of WH-Clefts and IT-Clefts in discourse.' *Language 54*. 4. 883-901.

Quirk, R., S. Greenbaum, G. Leech, and J. Svartvik. 1985. *A Comprehensive Grammar of the English Language*. London: Longman

Quirk, R. and S. Greenbaum. 1990. *A Student's Grammar of the English Language.* London: Longman

Rodney, H. 1984. *Introduction to the Grammar of English*. Cambridge University Press

Steer, J. and K. Carlisi. 1997. *The Advanced Grammar Book. 2nd ed.* Heinle & Heknle Publishers.

Swan, M. and C. Walter. 1997. *How English Works a grammar practice book.* Oxford University Press.

Sweet, H. 1981. *A New English Grammar*. Oxford University Press

Thomson, A. J. and A. V. Martinet. 1986. *A Practical English Grammar, Exercises 1-2*. Oxford: University Press

Index

A

B

C

D

Q

R

S

T

U

V